AL LEONARD

ITAR METHOD

lement to Any Pedal Steel
Guitar Method

PEDAL STEEL GUITAR SONGBOOK

For E9 Tuning

BY JOHNIE HELMS

T0039770

PLAYBACK+
Speed • Pitch • Balance • Loop

To access audio visit:
www.halleonard.com/mylibrary

2818-7625-7892-0432

ISBN 978-1-4234-9849-0

7777 W. BLUEMOUND RD. P.O. BOX 13819 MILWAUKEE, WI 53213

Visit Hal Leonard Online at
www.halleonard.com

SONG STRUCTURE

The songs in this book have different sections, which may or may not include the following:

Intro

This is usually a short instrumental section that "introduces" the song at the beginning.

Verse

This is one of the main sections of a song and conveys most of the storyline. A song usually has several verses, all with the same music but each with different lyrics.

Chorus

This is often the most memorable section of a song. Unlike the verse, the chorus usually has the same lyrics every time it repeats.

Bridge

This section is a break from the rest of the song, often having a very different chord progression and feel.

Solo

This is an instrumental section, often played over the verse or chorus structure.

Outro

Similar to an intro, this section brings the song to an end.

ENDINGS & REPEATS

Many of the songs have some new symbols that you must understand before playing. Each of these represents a different type of ending.

1st and 2nd Endings

These are indicated by brackets and numbers. The first time through a song section, play the first ending and then repeat. The second time through, skip the first ending, and play through the second ending.

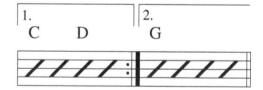

D.S.

This means "Dal Segno" or "from the sign." When you see this abbreviation above the staff, find the sign (𝄋) earlier in the song and resume playing from that point.

al Coda

This means "to the Coda," a concluding section in the song. If you see the words "D.S. al Coda," return to the sign (𝄋) earlier in the song and play until you see the words "To Coda," then skip to the Coda at the end of the song, indicated by the symbol: ⊕.

al Fine

This means "to the end." If you see the words "D.S. al Fine," return to the sign (𝄋) earlier in the song and play until you see the word "Fine."

D.C.

This means "Da Capo" or "from the head." When you see this abbreviation above the staff, return to the beginning (or "head") of the song and resume playing.

CONTENTS

LOVE ME TENDER

Words and Music by
ELVIS PRESLEY and VERA MATSON

Verse

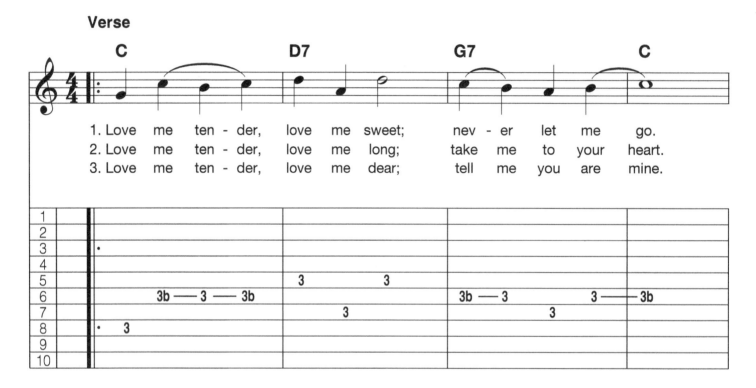

1. Love me ten - der, love me sweet; nev - er let me go.
2. Love me ten - der, love me long; take me to your heart.
3. Love me ten - der, love me dear; tell me you are mine.

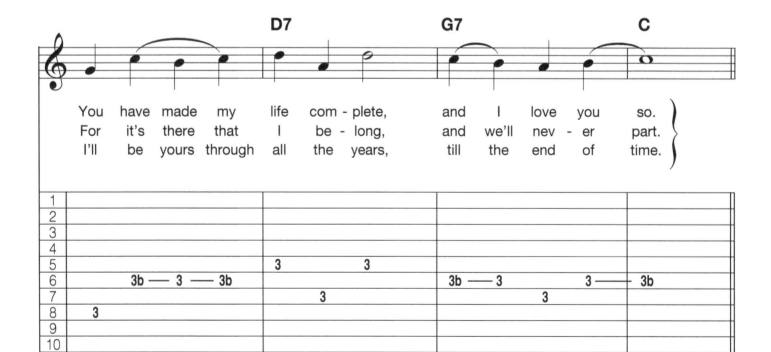

You have made my life com - plete, and I love you so.
For it's there that I be - long, and we'll nev - er part.
I'll be yours through all the years, till the end of time.

Chorus

C   E7   Am   C7   F   Fm

Love me ten - der, love me true, all my dreams ful -

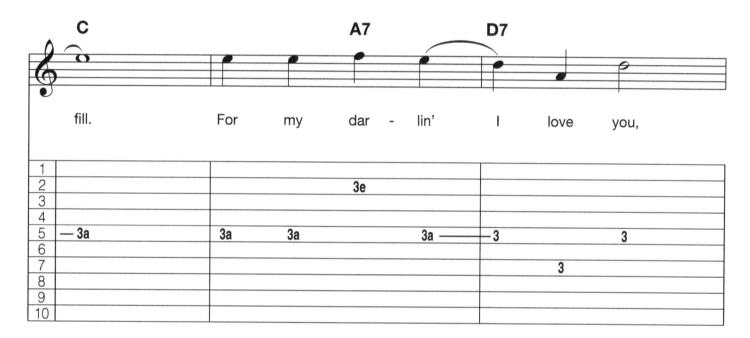

C   A7   D7

fill. For my dar - lin' I love you,

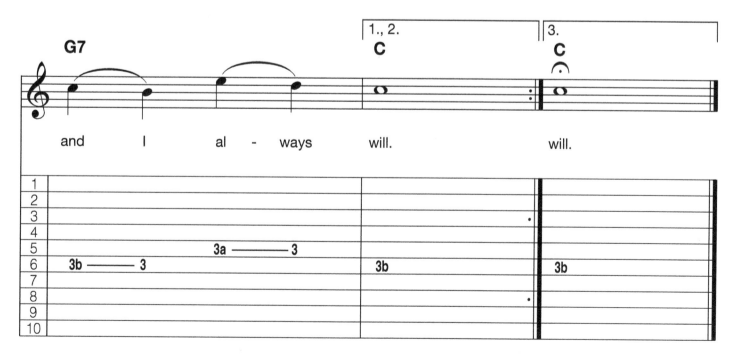

G7   C   C

and I al - ways will. will.

LET IT BE

Words and Music by JOHN LENNON
and PAUL McCARTNEY

Verse

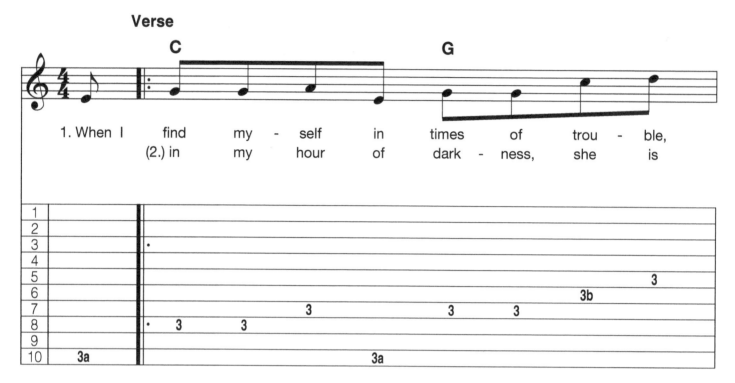

1. When I find my - self in times of trou - ble,
(2.) in my hour of dark - ness, she is

moth - er Mar - y comes to me,
stand - ing right in front of me,
speak - ing words of wis - dom, let it

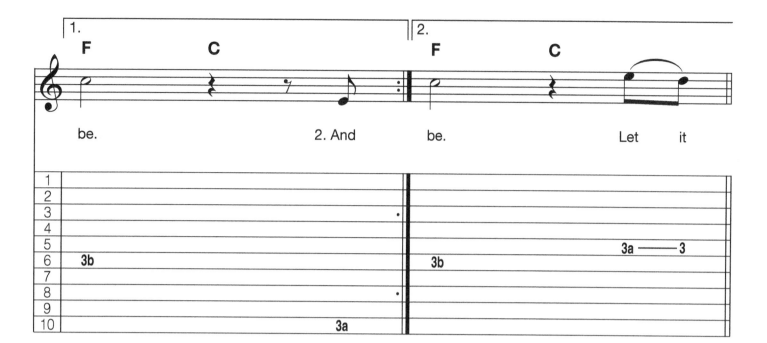

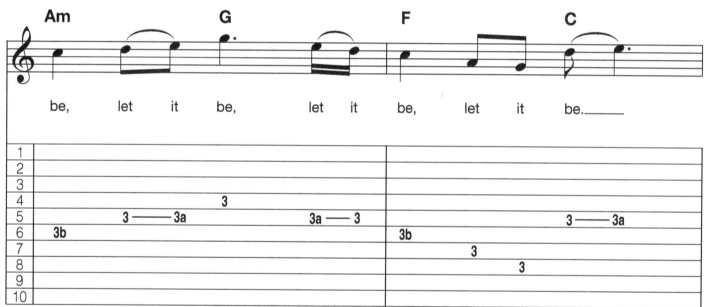

Chorus

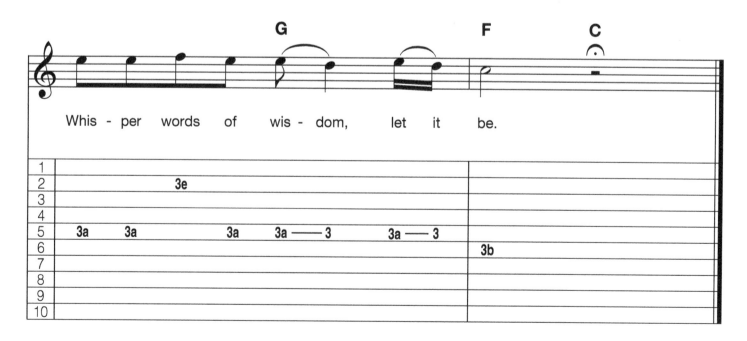

STEEL GUITAR RAG

Words by
MERLE TRAVIS and CLIFF STONE
Music by
LEON McAULIFFE

Verse

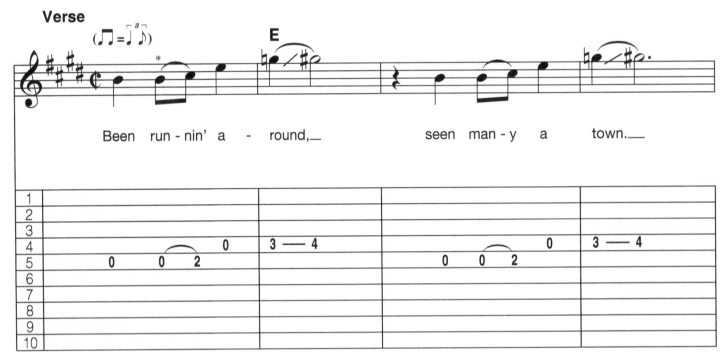

* **Hammer-on**: sound note by plucking open string and
touching string with bar at indicated fret.

** **Pull-off**: lift bar off string to sound
open-string note.

Copyright © 1941 by Bourne Co. (ASCAP)
Copyright Renewed
International Copyright Secured All Rights Reserved

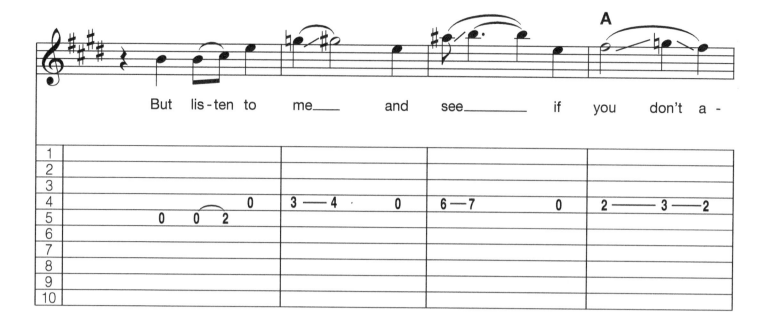

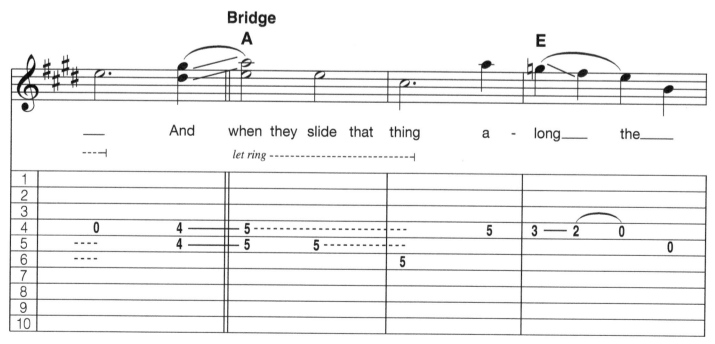

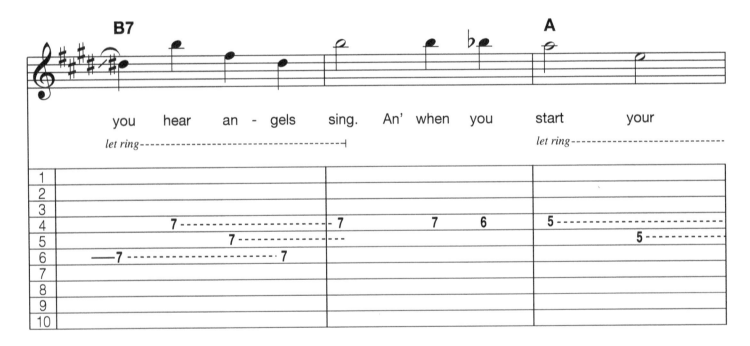

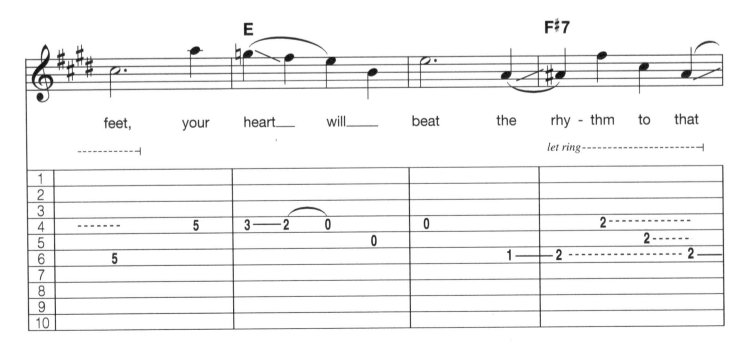

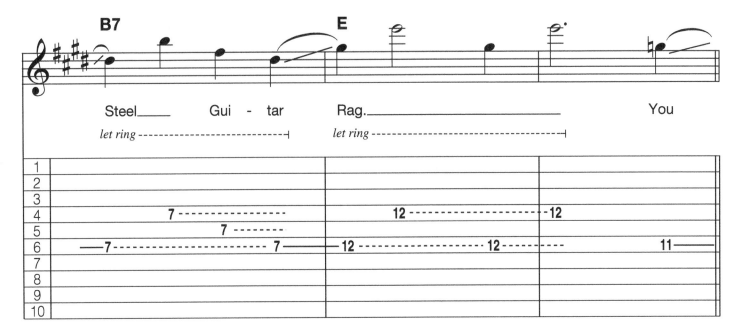

Steel___ Gui - tar Rag._____ You

let ring ----------------------------⌐   *let ring* ----------------------------⌐

1						
2						
3						
4		7-----------		12---------------12		
5		7--------				
6	—7----------------7—		12------------------12-----		11—	
7						
8						
9						
10						

Chorus

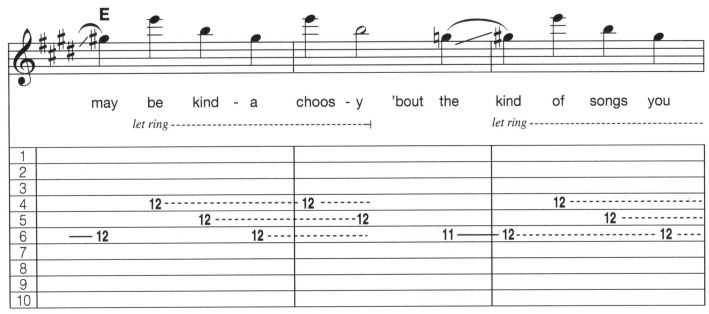

may be kind - a choos - y 'bout the kind of songs you_____

let ring ---------------------------------⌐   *let ring* ------------------------------

1						
2						
3						
4		12------------12--------				12--------------------
5		12---------------12				12-------------
6	—12	12-----------		11—	12---------------12----	
7						
8						
9						
10						

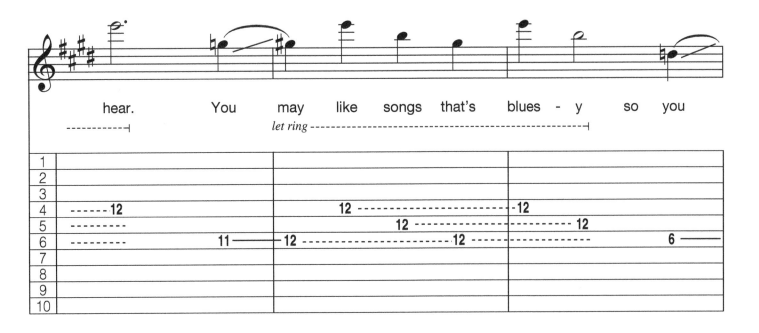

hear. You may like songs that's blues - y so you

----------⌐   *let ring* ---⌐

1				
2				
3				
4	------12		12-----------------------12	
5	--------		12----------------------12	
6	--------	11—	12------------------12----------------	6—
7				
8				
9				
10				

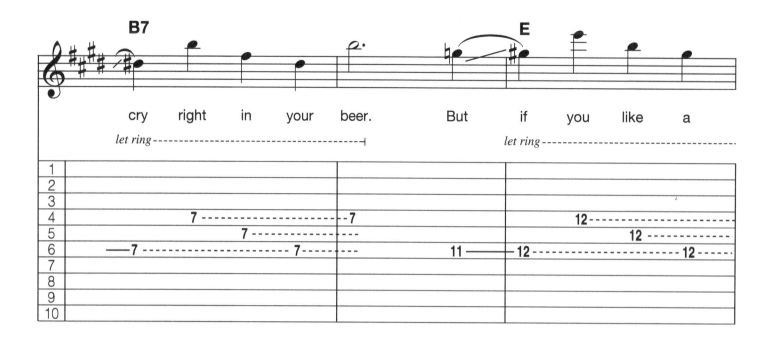

cry right in your beer. But if you like a

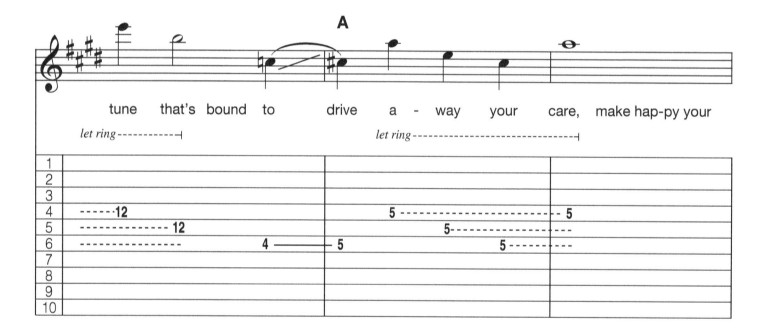

tune that's bound to drive a - way your care, make hap-py your

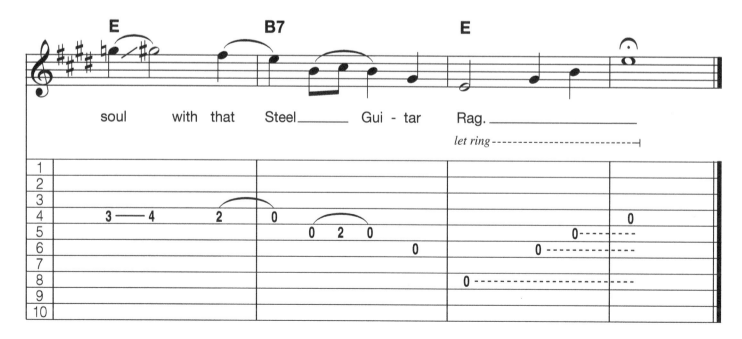

soul with that Steel____ Gui - tar Rag.____

THE HOUSE OF THE RISING SUN

Words and Music by
ALAN PRICE

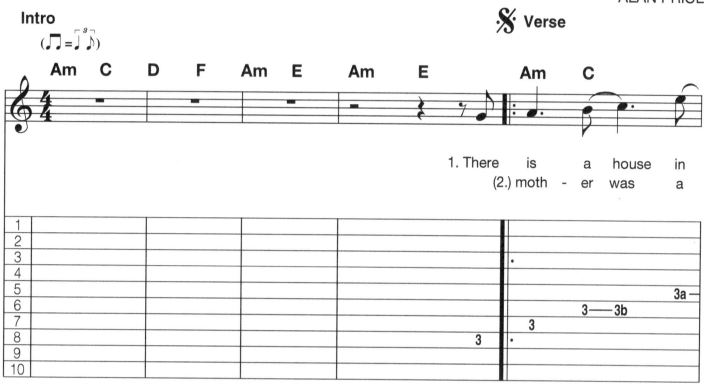

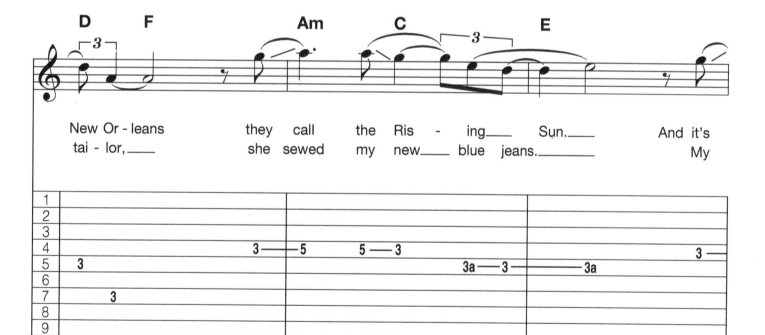

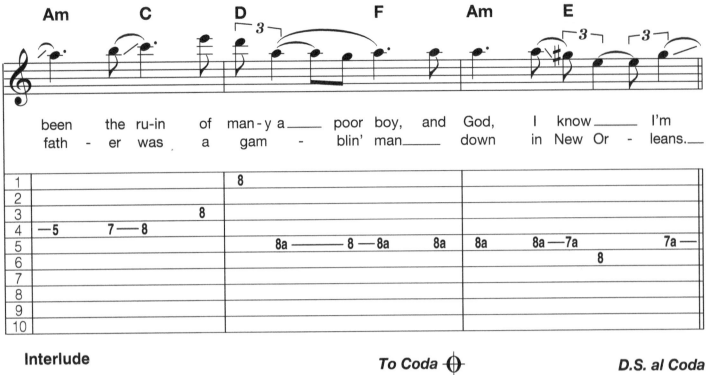

been the ru-in of man-y a ___ poor boy, and God, I know ___ I'm
fath - er was a gam - blin' man ___ down in New Or - leans. ___

Interlude   **To Coda** ⊕   **D.S. al Coda**

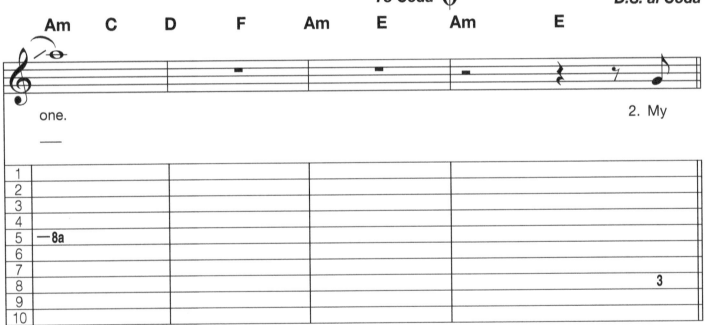

one.

2. My

⊕ **Coda**

STAND BY ME

Words and Music by JERRY LEIBER,
MIKE STOLLER and BEN E. KING

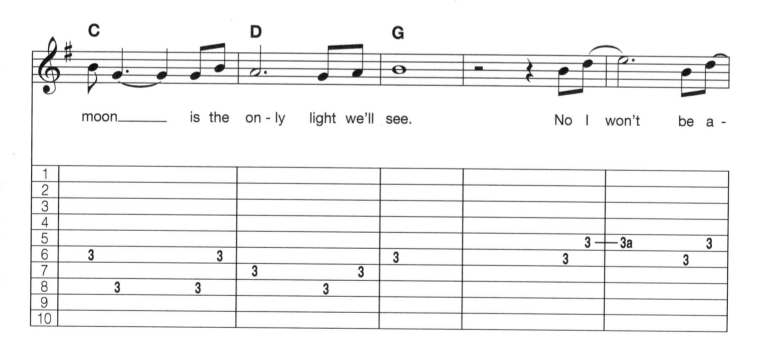

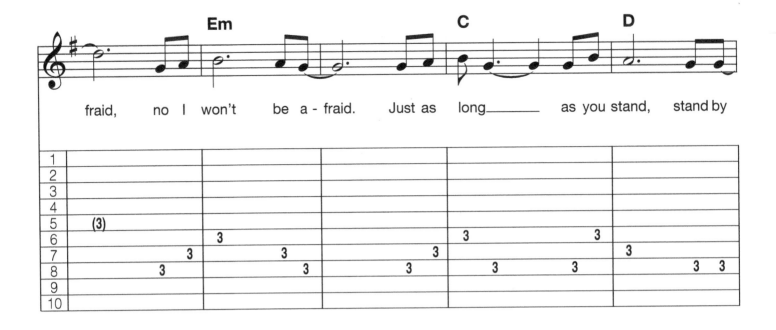

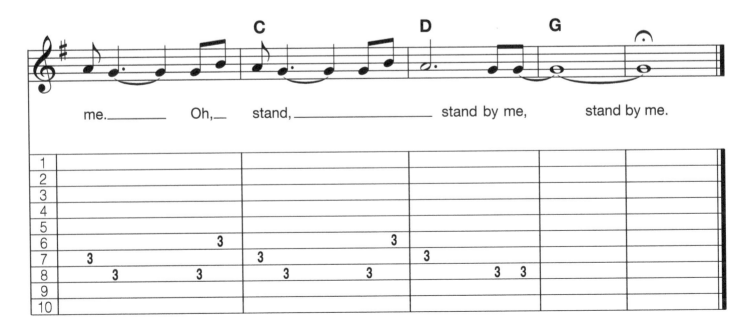

NOWHERE MAN

Words and Music by
JOHN LENNON and PAUL McCARTNEY

Chorus

He's a real no-where man, sit-ting in his

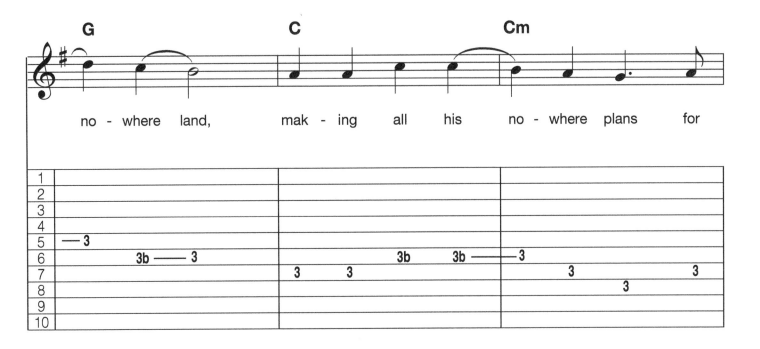

no-where land, mak-ing all his no-where plans for

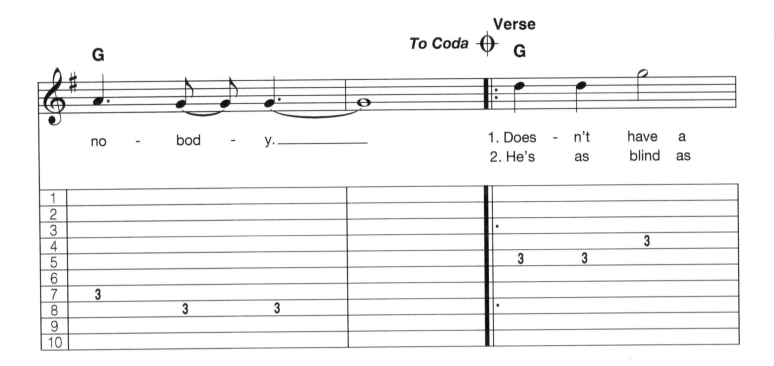

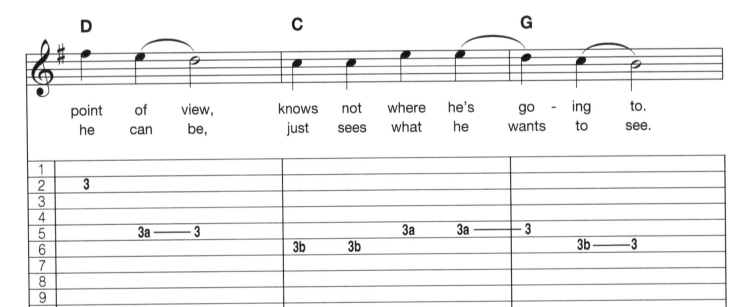

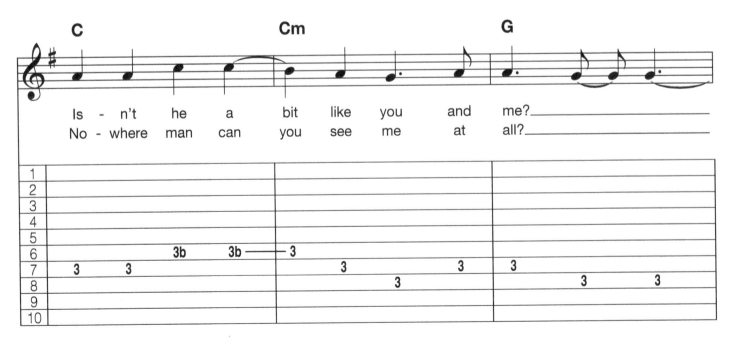

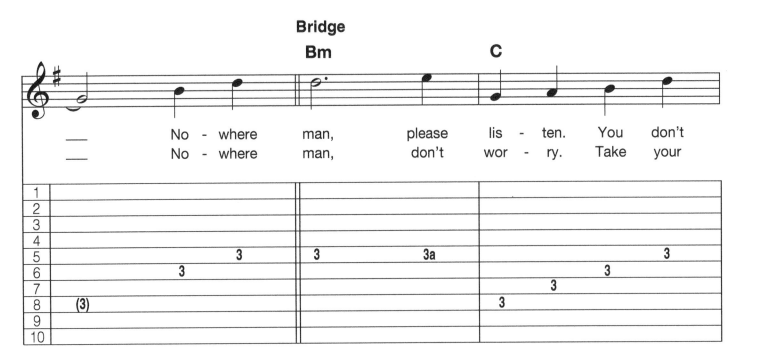

Bridge

No - where man, please lis - ten. You don't
No - where man, don't wor - ry. Take your

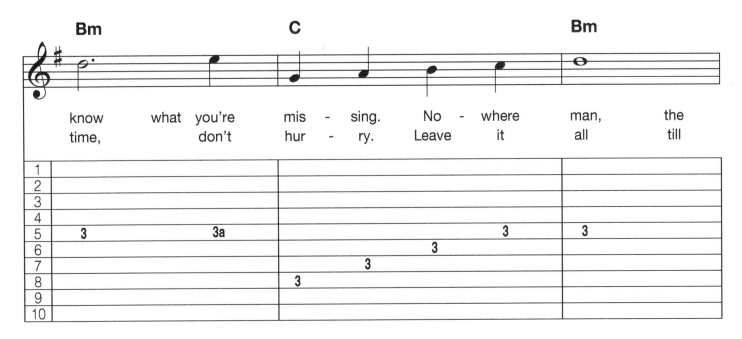

know what you're mis - sing. No - where man, the
time, don't hur - ry. Leave it all till

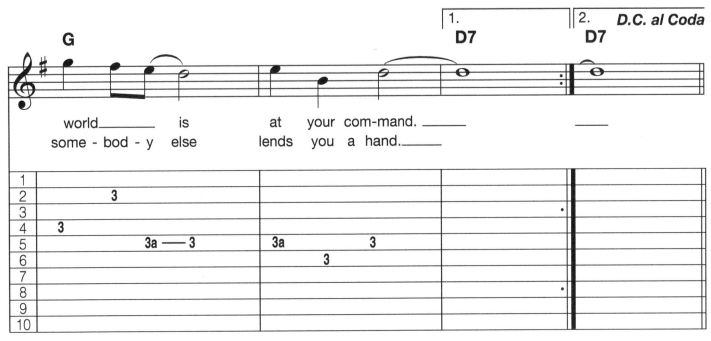

world_____ is at your com-mand. _____ _____
some - bod - y else lends you a hand._____

19

SLEEPWALK

By SANTO FARINA,
JOHN FARINA and ANN FARINA

Intro

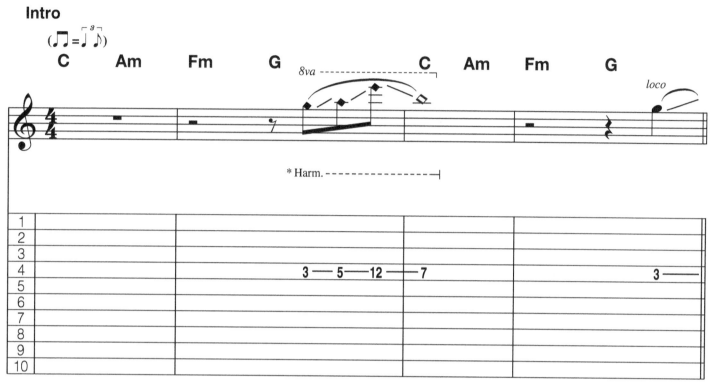

*Lightly touch fourth string with R.H. palm
at 15th fret while plucking to create harmonic.

Verse

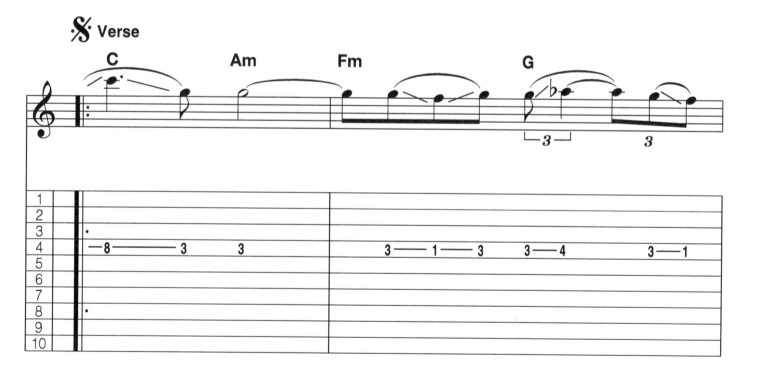

To Coda ⊕

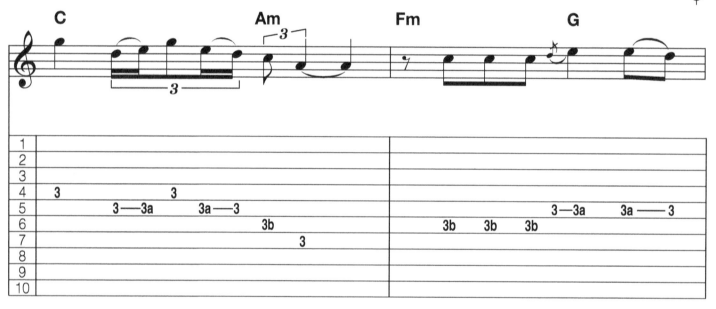

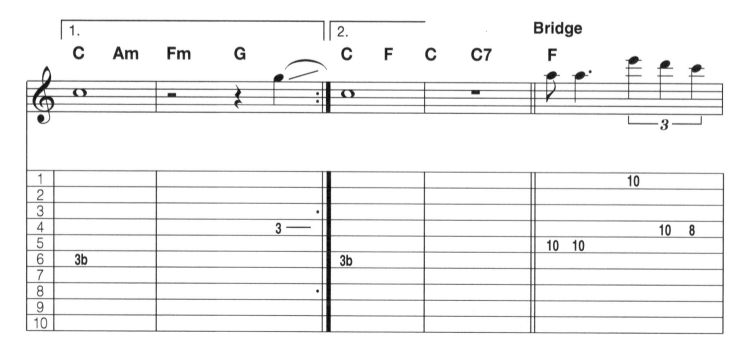

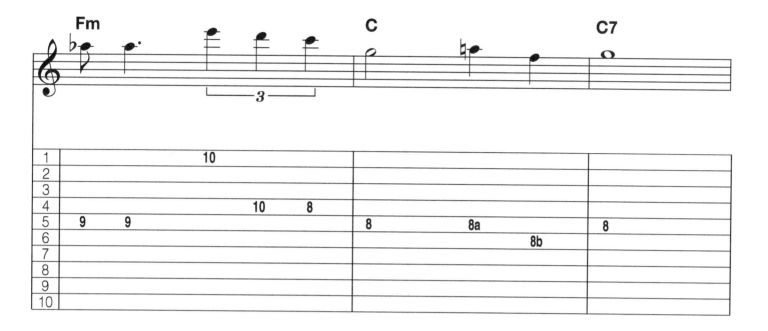

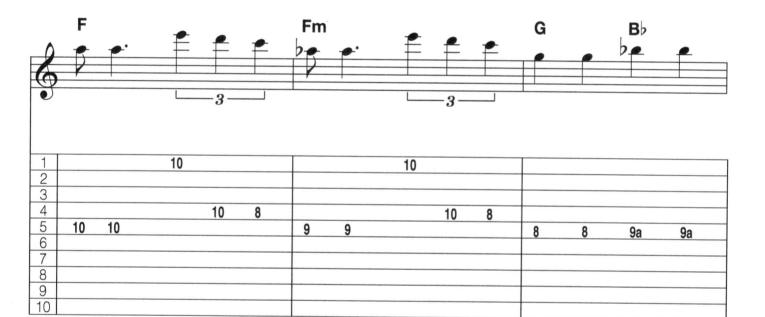

D.S. al Coda   **Coda**

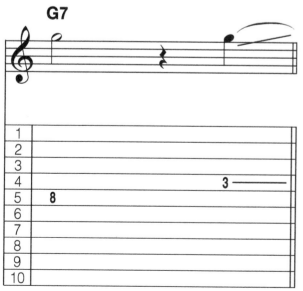

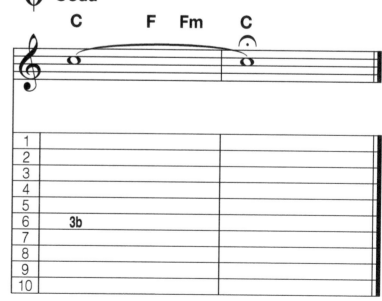

YOUR CHEATIN' HEART

Words and Music by
HANK WILLIAMS

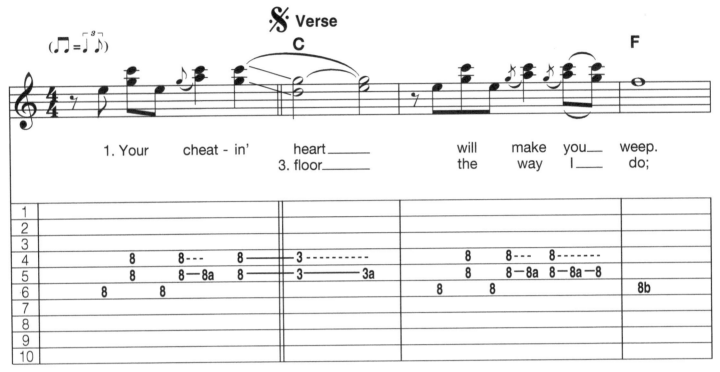

1. Your cheat - in' heart _____ will make you_ weep.
3. floor_____ the way I___ do;

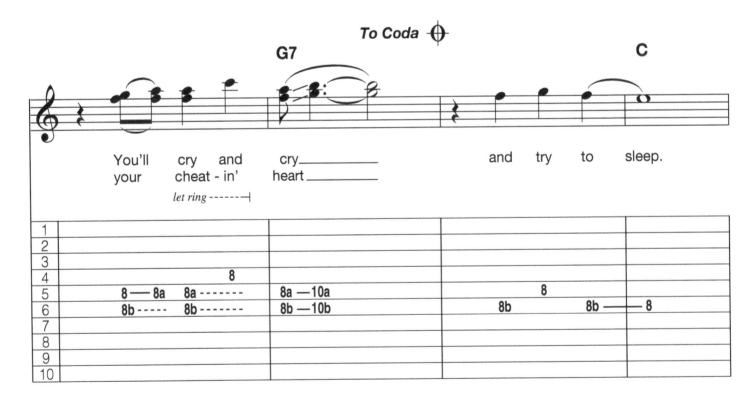

You'll cry and cry_____ and try to sleep.
your cheat - in' heart _____

let ring -------

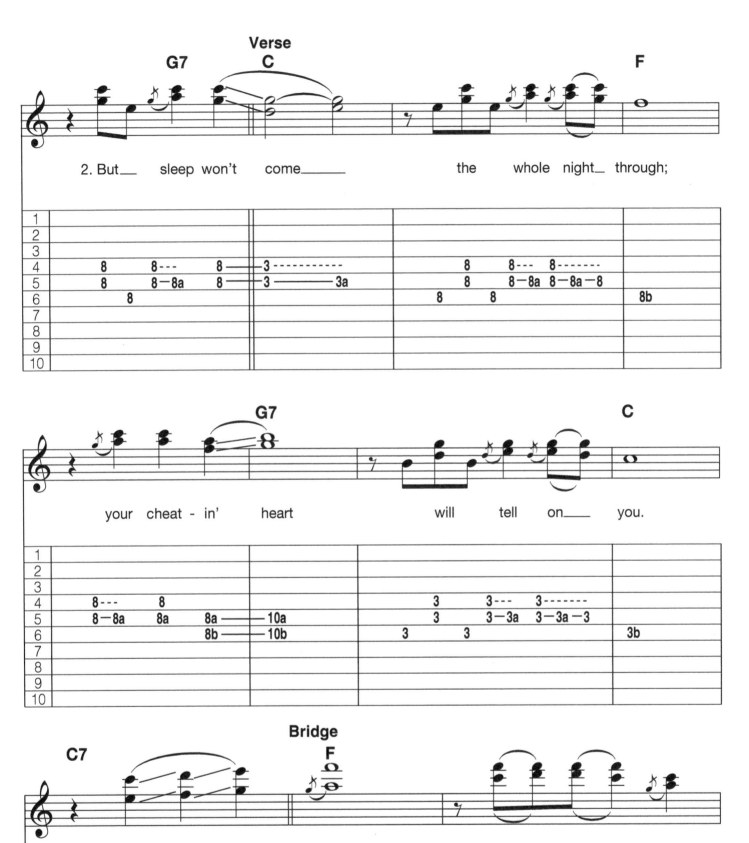

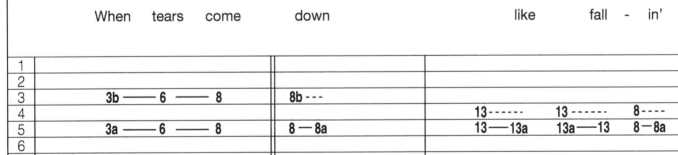

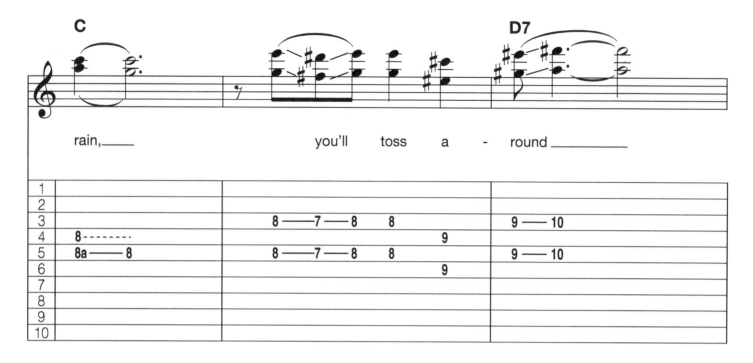

rain,_____   you'll   toss   a - round _____

1			
2			
3		8 —7— 8 8	9 — 10
4	8--------	9	
5	8a —— 8	8 —7— 8 8	9 — 10
6		9	
7			
8			
9			
10			

D.S. al Coda

and   call   my   name.   3. You'll   walk   the

1			
2			
3			
4	10 10----- 10		8 8--- 8 ——
5	10 10—10a 10		8 8 —8a 8 ——
6	10	10b	8
7			
8			
9			
10			

⊕ Coda

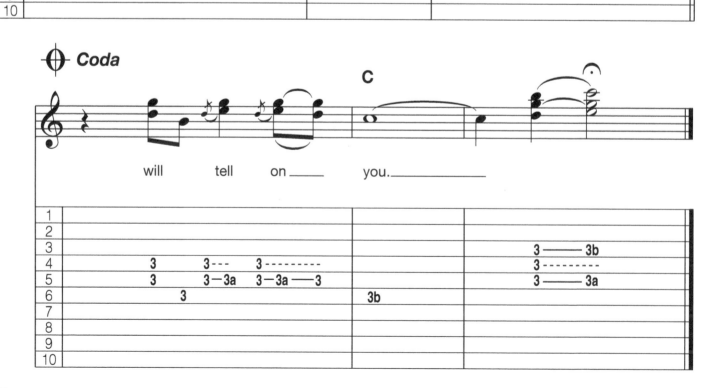

will   tell   on ____   you._____

1			
2			
3			3 —— 3b
4	3 3--- 3---------		3---------
5	3 3—3a 3—3a —3		3 —— 3a
6	3	3b	
7			
8			
9			
10			

KING OF THE ROAD

Words and Music by
ROGER MILLER

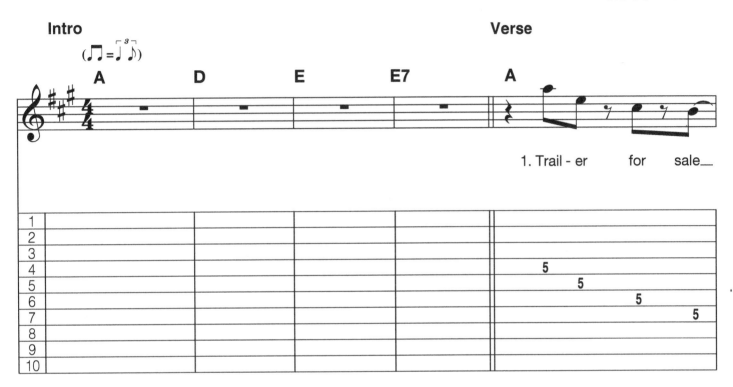

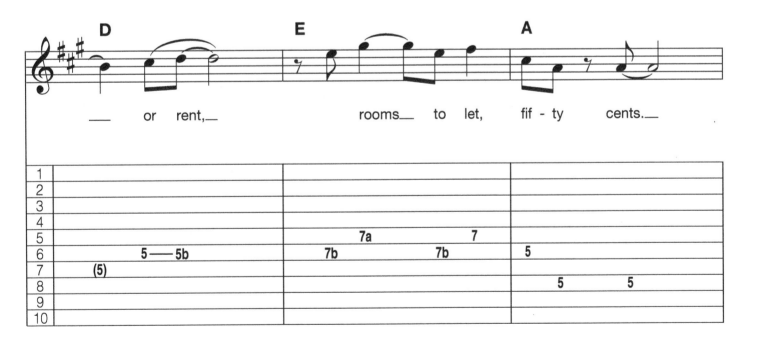

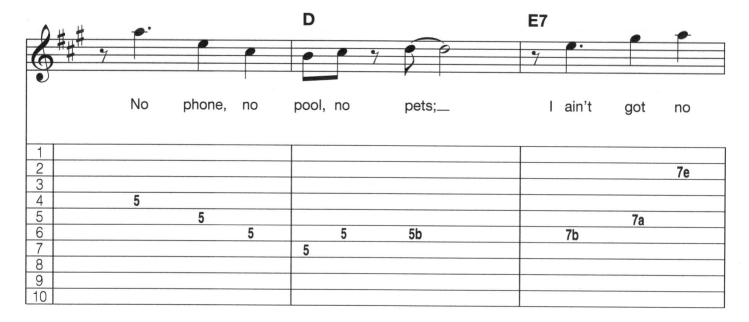

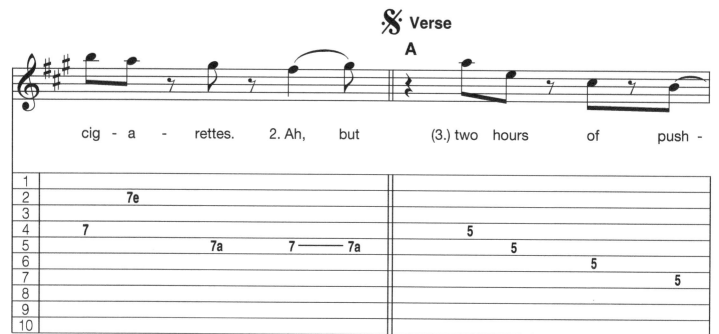

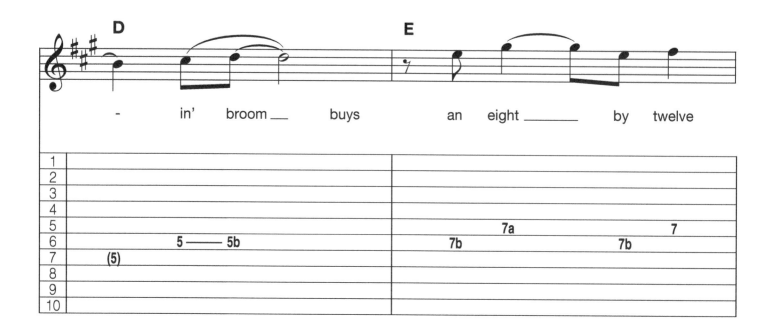

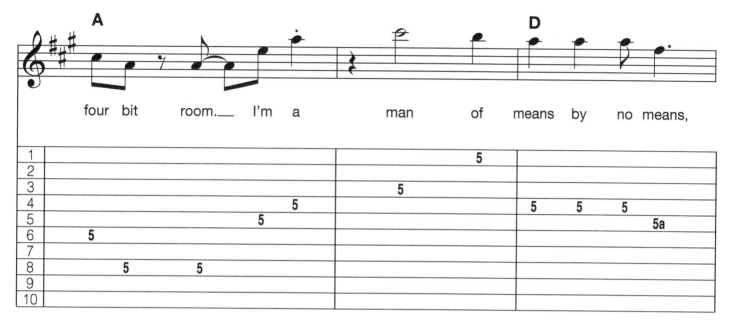

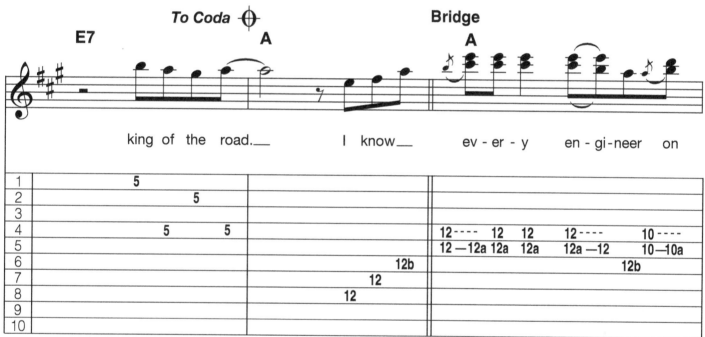

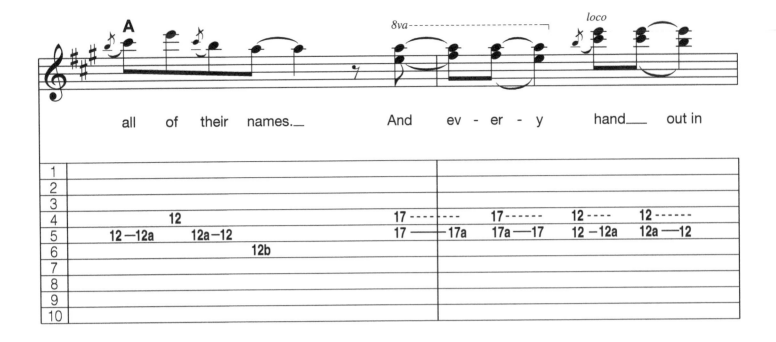

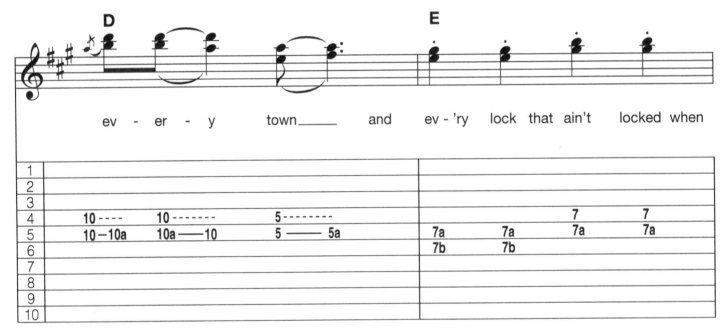

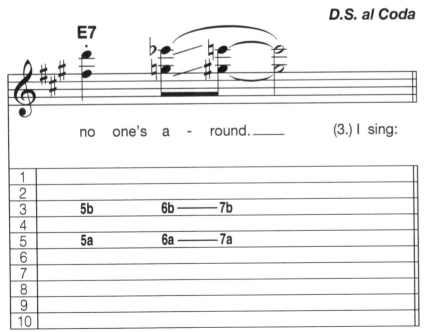

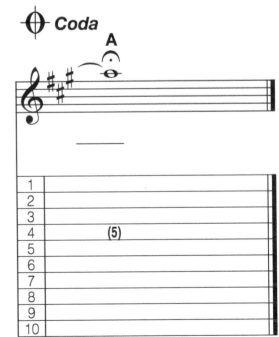

LAST DATE

By FLOYD CRAMER

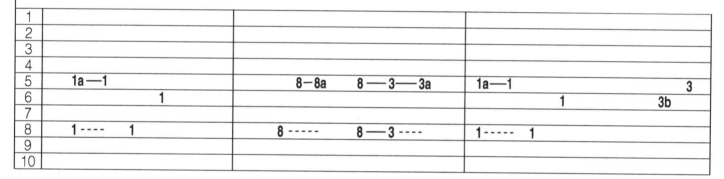

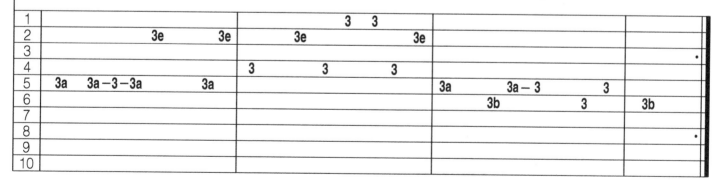

Bridge

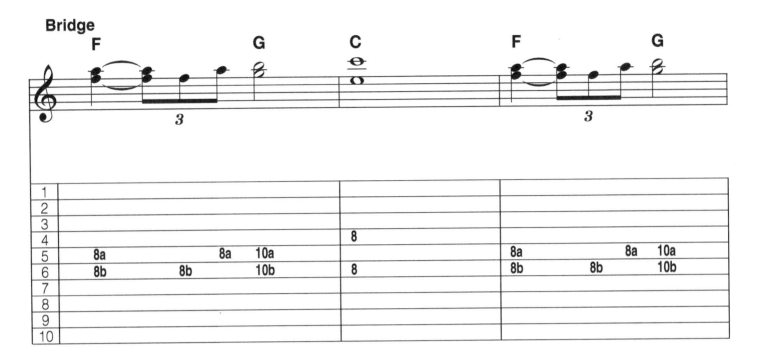

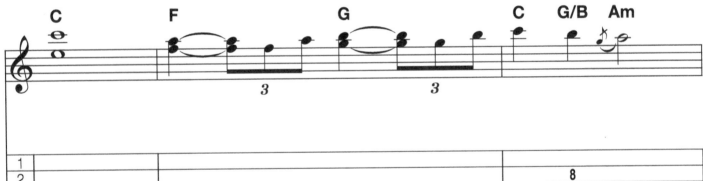

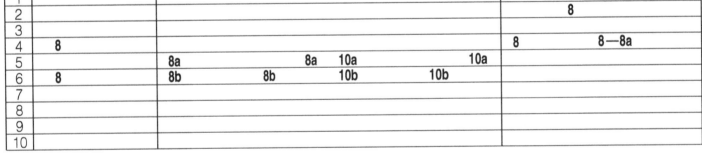

D.S. al Coda

Coda

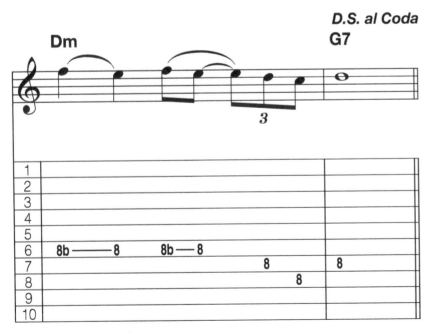

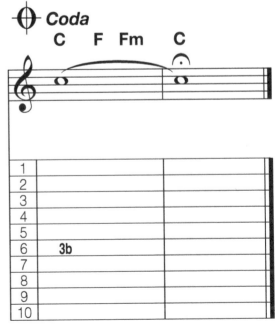

32

MY GIRL

Words and Music by
WILLIAM "SMOKEY" ROBINSON
and RONALD WHITE

Intro

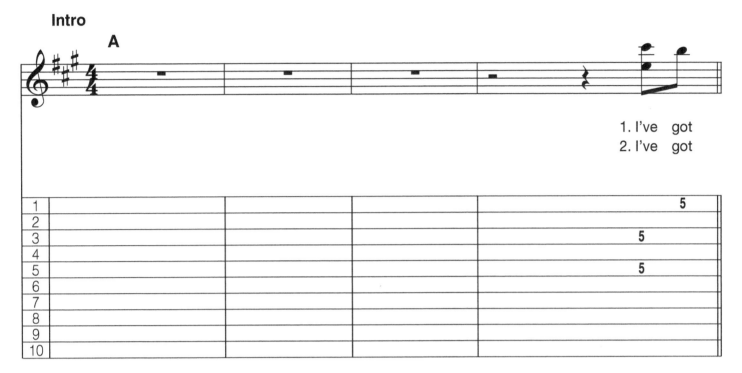

1. I've got
2. I've got

Verse

sun - shine   on   a   cloud - y   day.
so   much   hon-ey,   the   bees   en - vy   me.

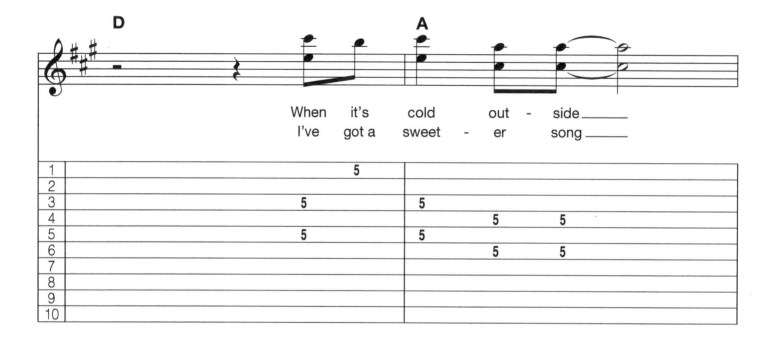

When   it's   cold   out - side_____
I've   got a   sweet - er   song_____

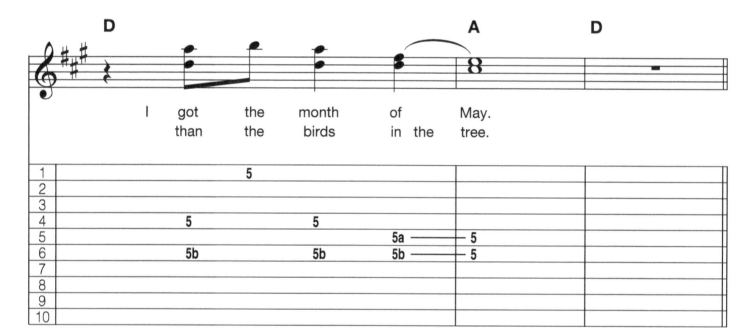

I   got   the   month   of   May.
than   the   birds   in the   tree.

Chorus

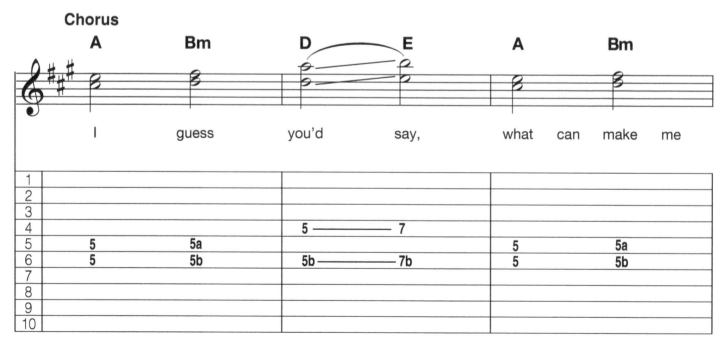

I   guess   you'd   say,   what   can   make   me

feel   this   way?   My   girl,   (my   girl,

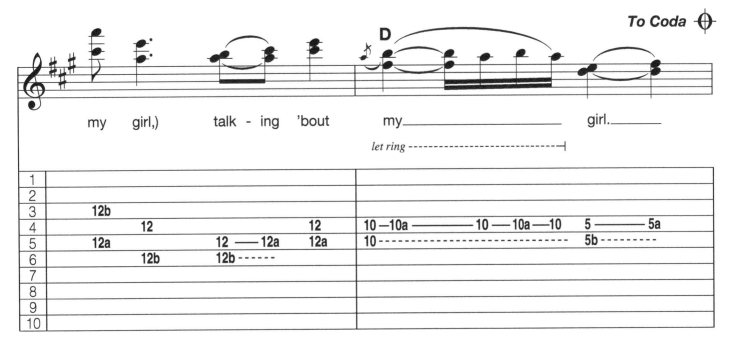

my   girl,)   talk - ing 'bout   my_____   girl._____

let ring --------------------------------|

To Coda ⊕

D.C. al Coda

(My   girl.)

⊕ **Coda**

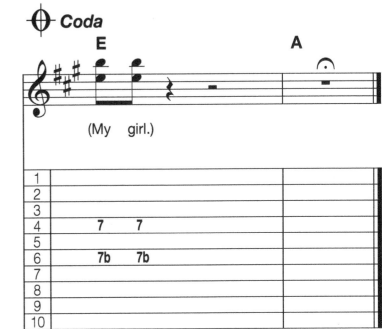

(My   girl.)

WHO'LL STOP THE RAIN

Words and Music by
JOHN FOGERTY

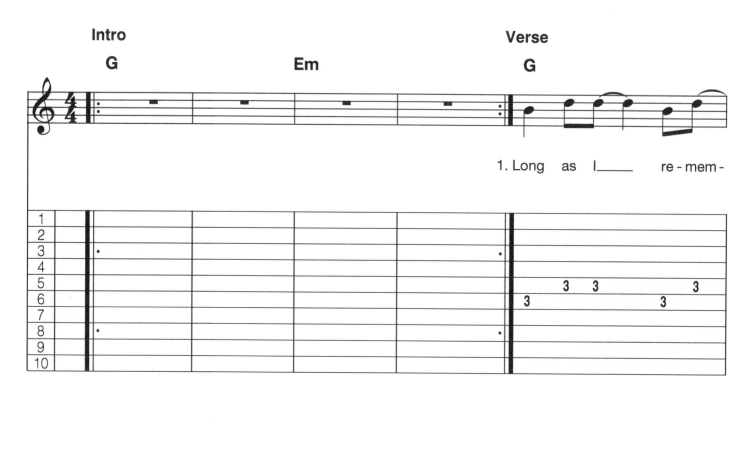

1. Long as I____ re - mem -

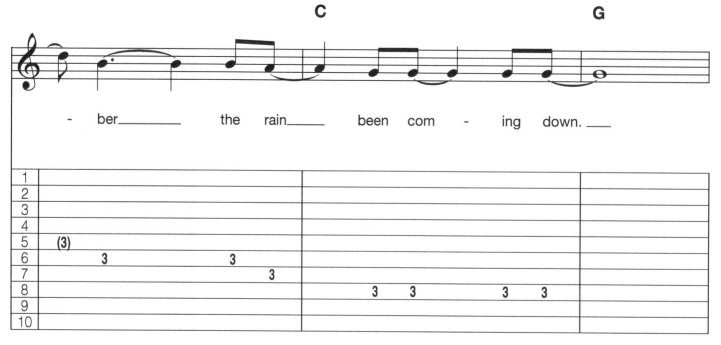

- ber_____ the rain____ been com - ing down. ___

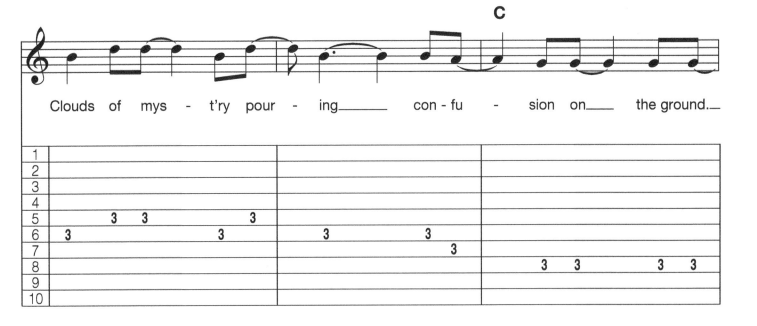

Clouds of mys - t'ry pour - ing___ con - fu - sion on___ the ground.___

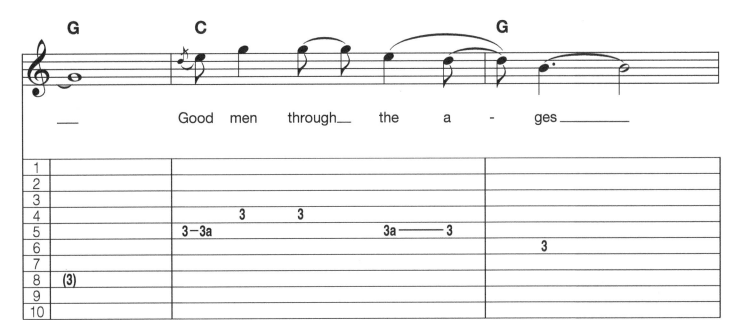

___ Good men through___ the a - ges___

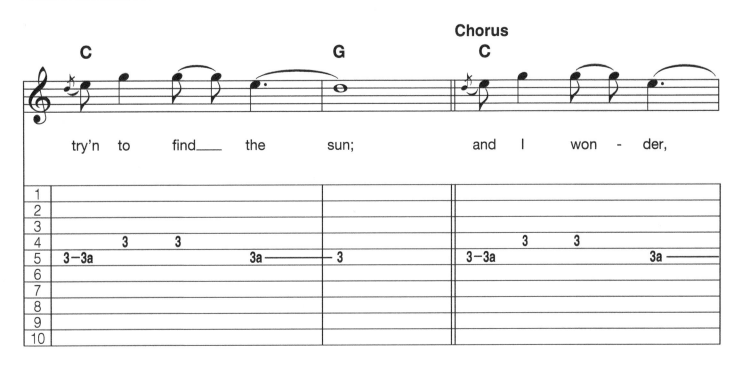

try'n to find___ the sun; and I won - der,

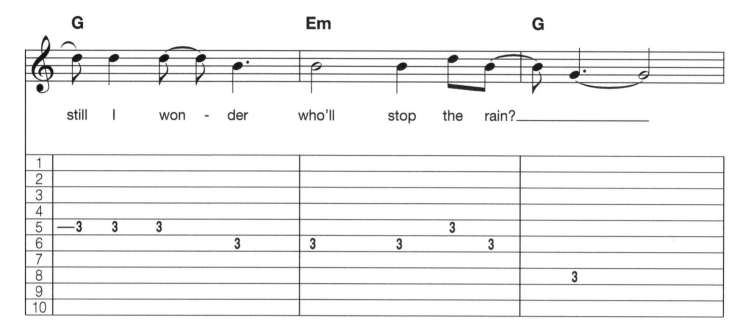

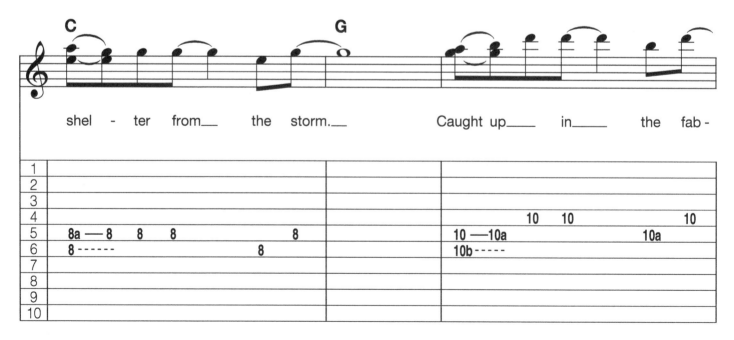

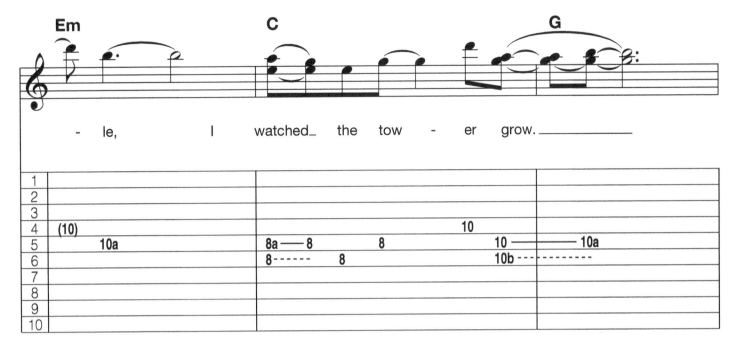

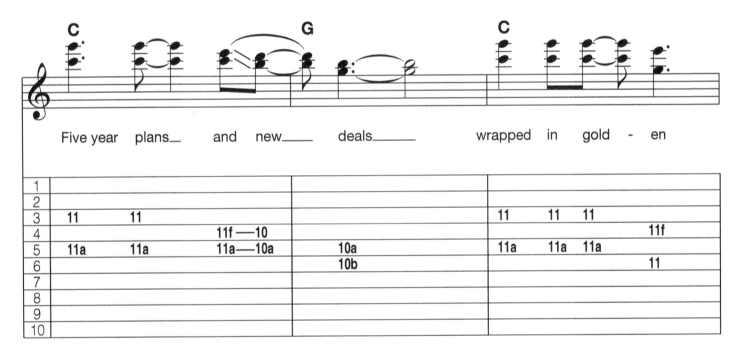

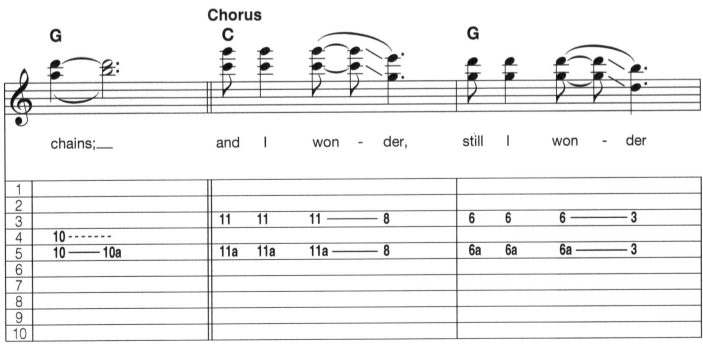

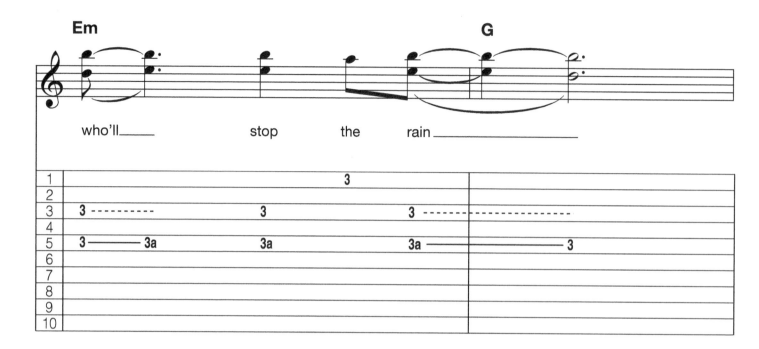

who'll_____   stop   the   rain _____

1				3		
2						
3	3 - - - - - - - - -		3		3 - - - - - - - - - - - - - - -	
4						
5	3 —— 3a		3a		3a —————— 3	
6						
7						
8						
9						
10						

And   I   won   -   der,   still   I   won   -   der

1						
2						
3	11	11	11 ————— 8	6	6	6 ————— 3
4						
5	11a	11a	11a ————— 8	6a	6a	6a ————— 3
6						
7						
8						
9						
10						

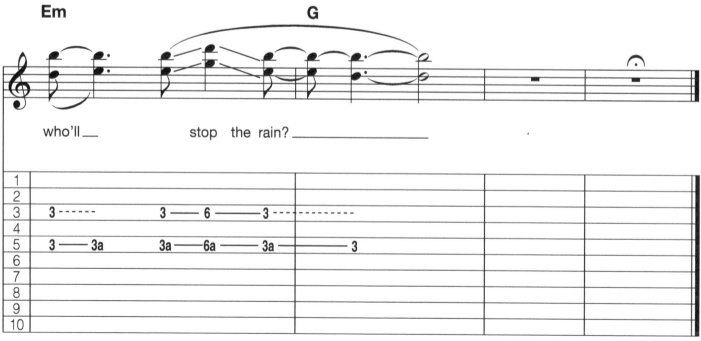

who'll __   stop   the   rain? _____

1				
2				
3	3 - - - - - -	3 — 6 — 3 - - - - - - - - - - -		
4				
5	3 — 3a	3a —6a —— 3a ——— 3		
6				
7				
8				
9				
10				

RELEASE ME

Words and Music by ROBERT YOUNT,
EDDIE MILLER and DUB WILLIAMS

Verse

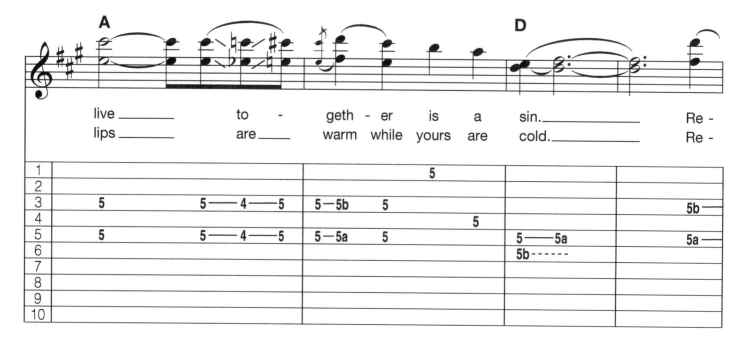

live _____ to - geth - er is a sin._____ Re -
lips _____ are _____ warm while yours are cold._____ Re -

lease me and let____ me love____ a - gain.
lease me dar - ling let____ me

Re - lease me dar - ling____ let____ me go.

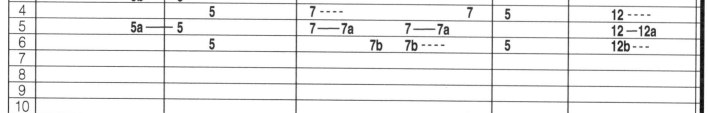

WILL THE CIRCLE BE UNBROKEN

Words by
ADA R. HABERSHON
Music by
CHARLES H. GABRIEL

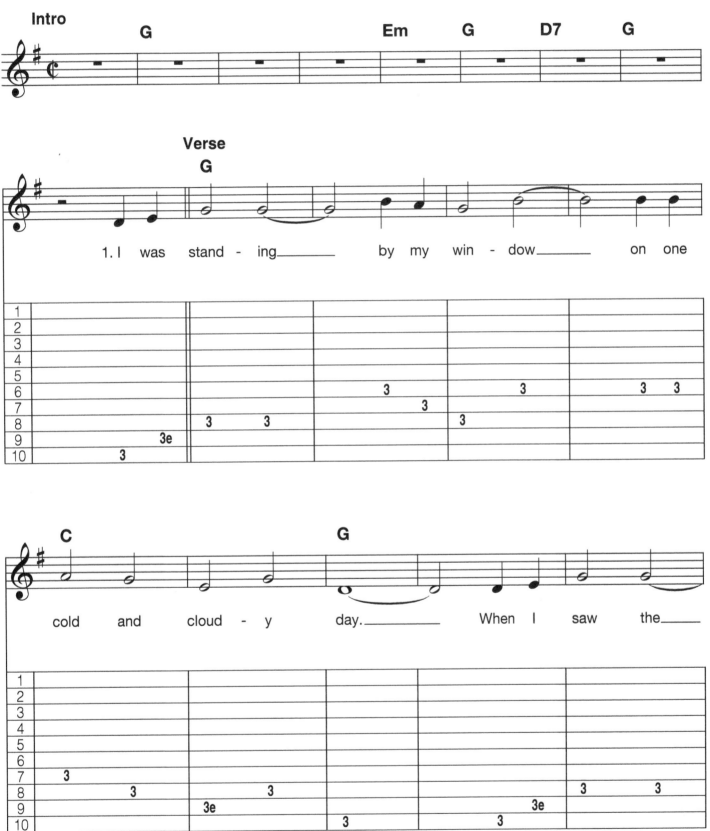

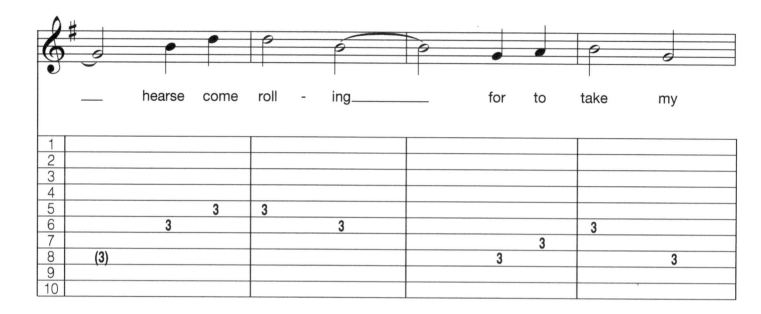

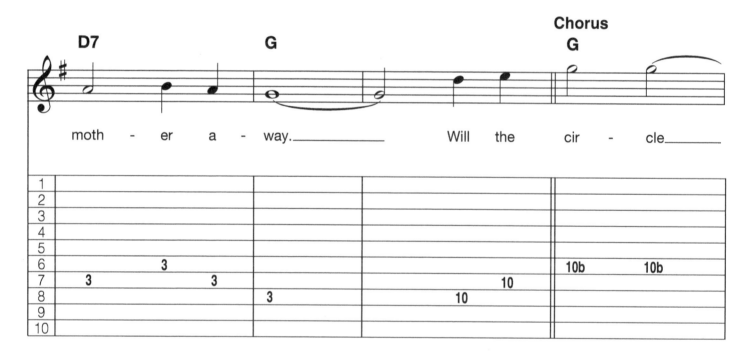

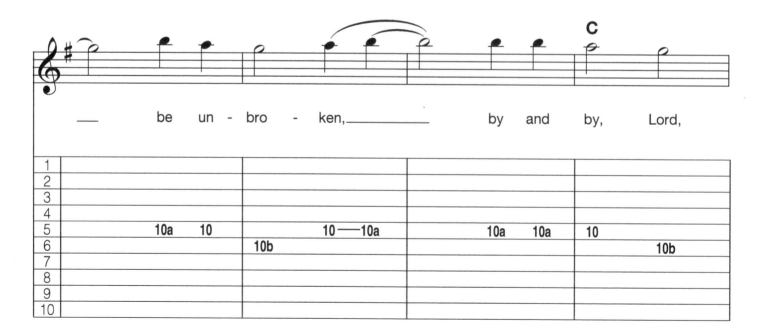

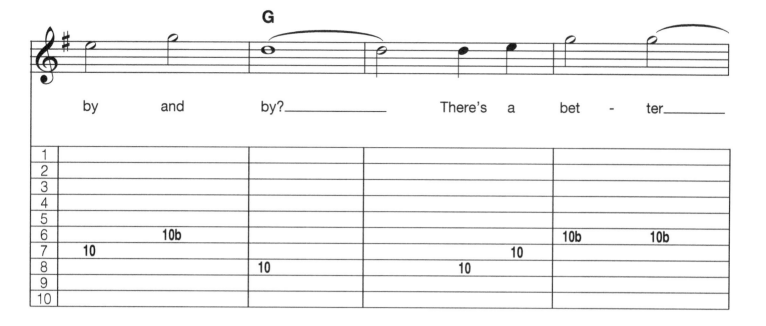

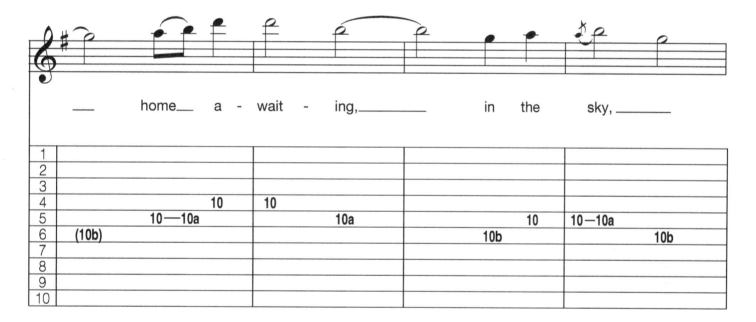

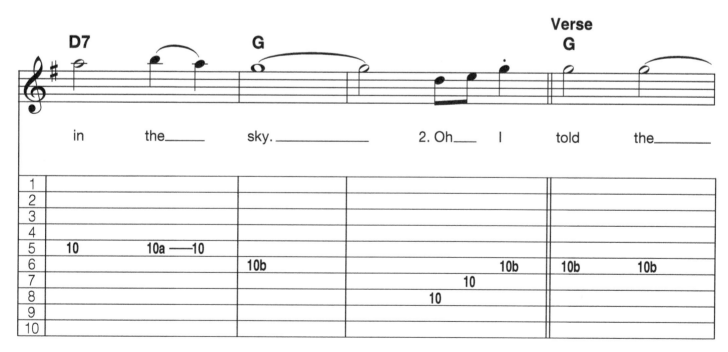

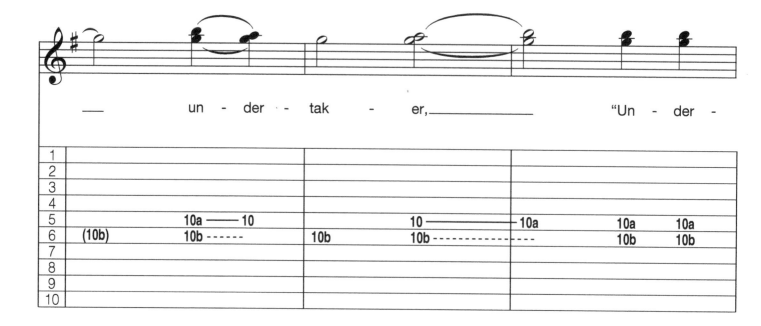

— un - der - tak - er,_____ "Un - der -

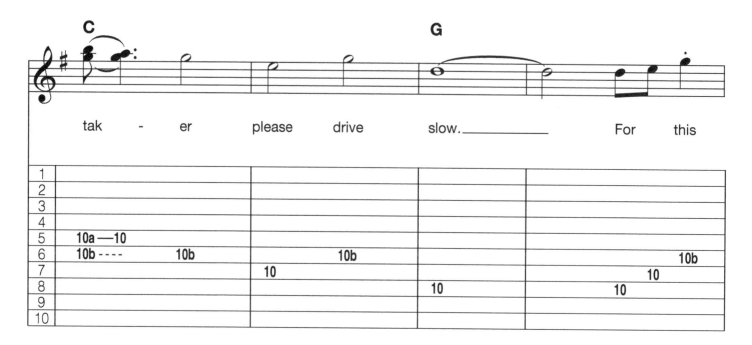

tak - er please drive slow._____ For this

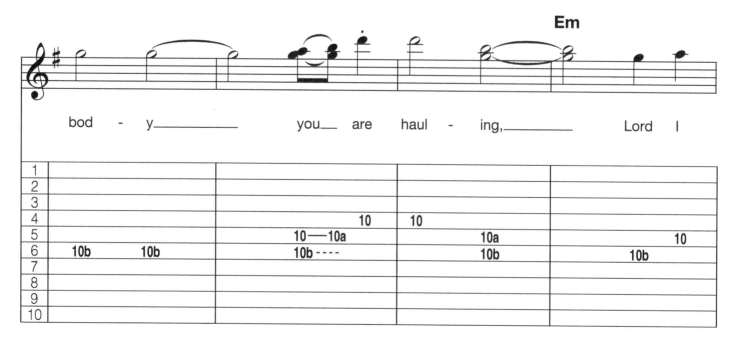

bod - y_____ you__ are haul - ing,_____ Lord I

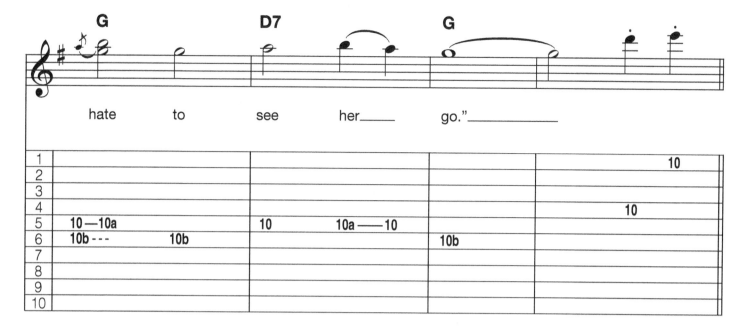

hate   to   see   her____   go."_____

Outro

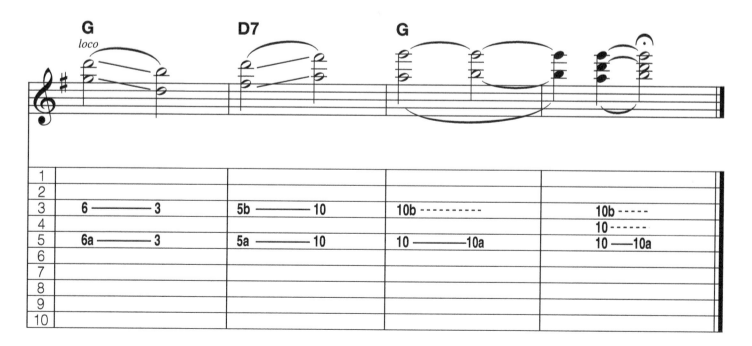

Teach Your Children

Words and Music by
GRAHAM NASH

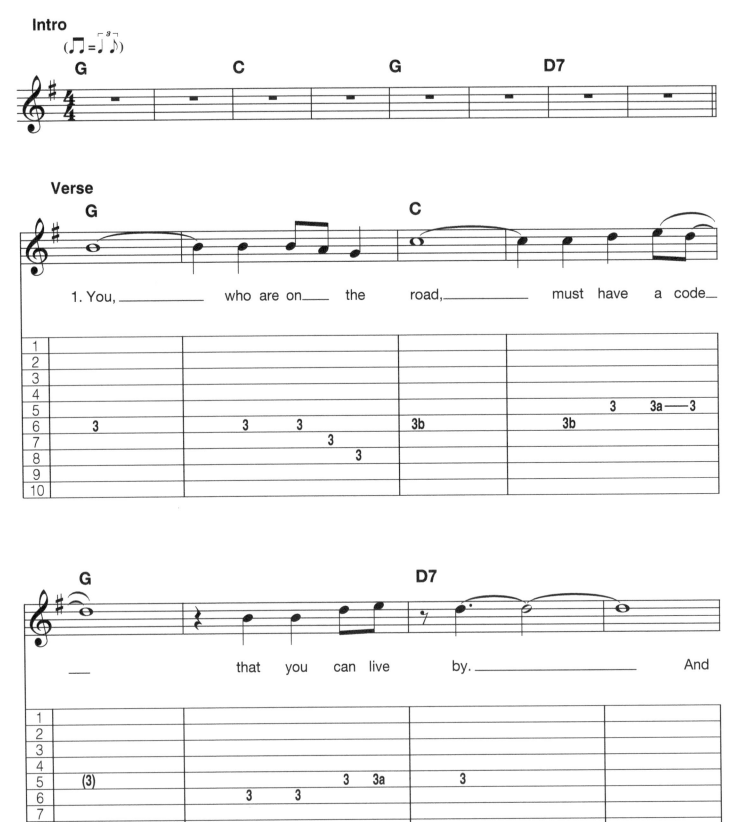

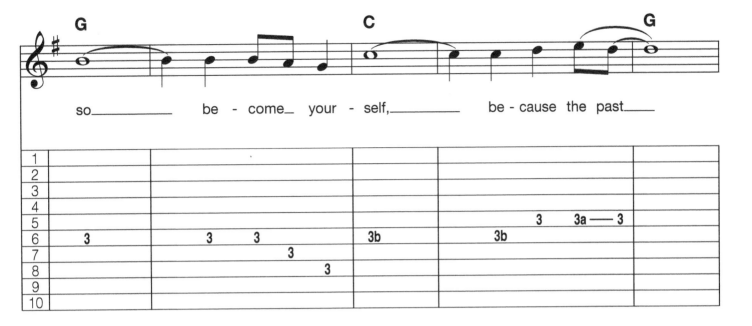

so_____ be - come_ your - self,_____ be - cause the past___

1							
2							
3							
4							
5							3 3a —— 3
6	3		3	3	3b	3b	
7			3				
8			3				
9							
10							

Chorus

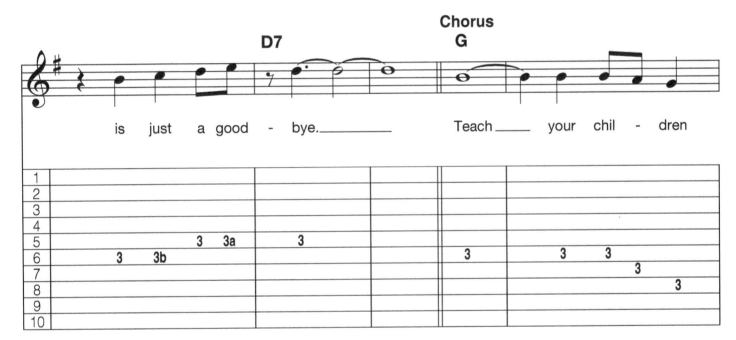

is   just   a   good - bye._____   Teach_____ your   chil - dren

1							
2							
3							
4							
5		3 3a	3				
6	3 3b				3	3 3	
7							3
8							3
9							
10							

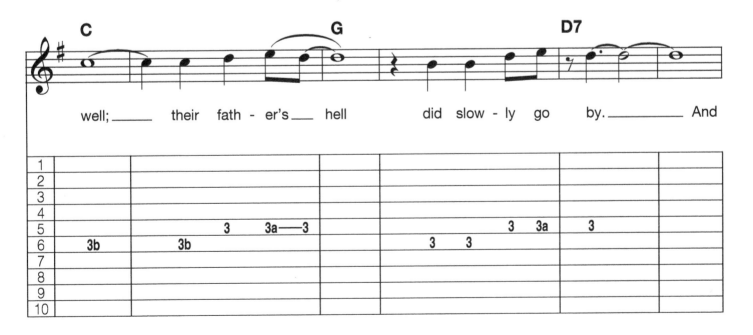

well;_____   their   fath - er's ___   hell   did   slow - ly   go   by. _____   And

1							
2							
3							
4							
5			3 3a — 3			3 3a	3
6	3b		3b		3 3		
7							
8							
9							
10							

feed_____ them on___ your dreams,_____ the one they picked,_

___ the one you'll know by. _____

Bridge

Don't you ev - er ask____ them why;_____ if they

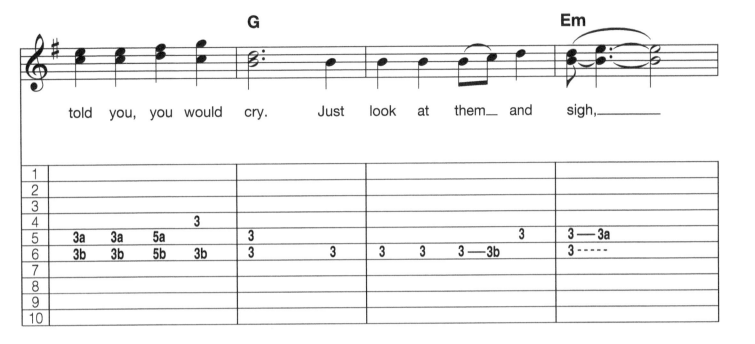

told you, you would cry. Just look at them— and sigh,_____

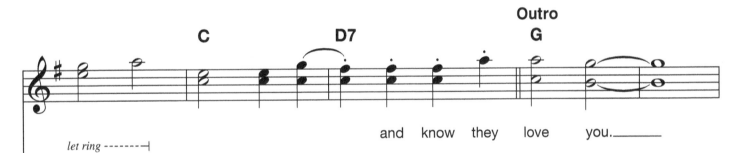

and know they love you._____

SWEET DREAMS

Words and Music by
DON GIBSON

Verse

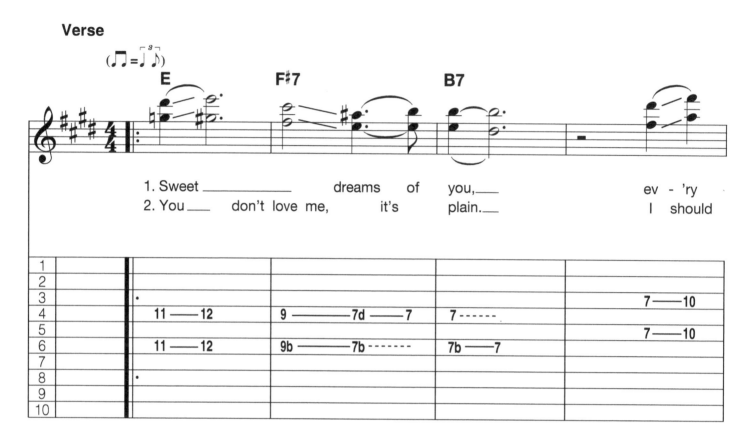

1. Sweet _____ dreams of you,___ ev - 'ry
2. You __ don't love me, it's plain.___ I should

night _____ I go__ through.___ Why
know,___ I'll nev - er wear your__ ring.___

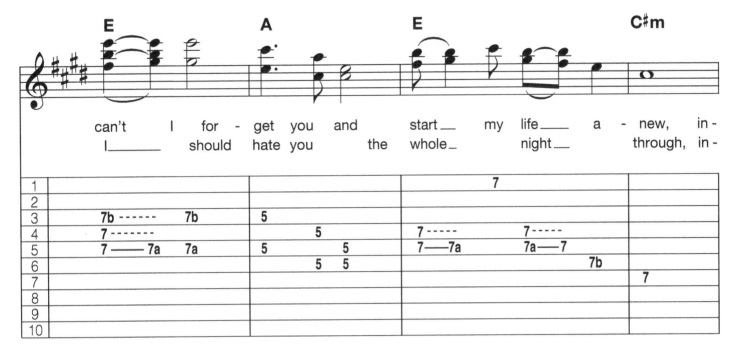

Outro

JAMBALAYA (ON THE BAYOU)

Words and Music by
HANK WILLIAMS

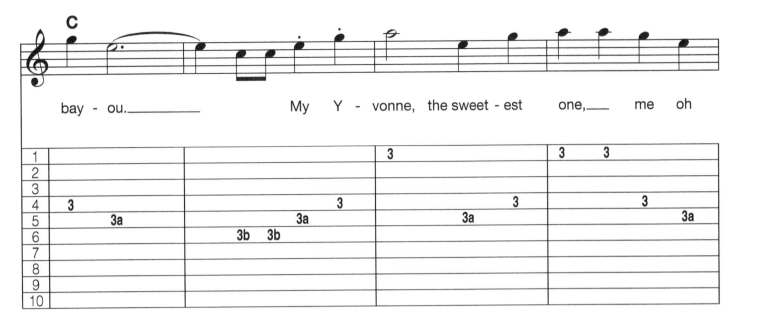

bay - ou._____ My Y - vonne, the sweet - est one,____ me oh

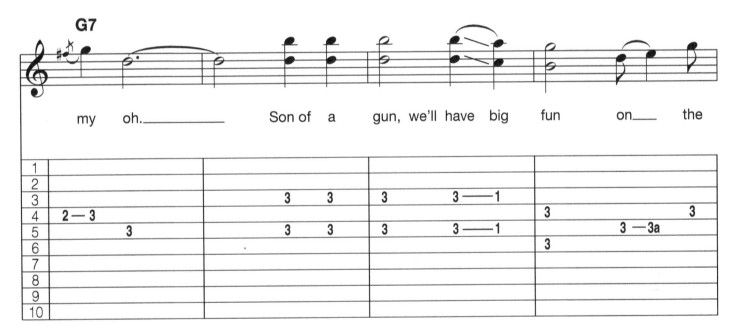

my oh._____ Son of a gun, we'll have big fun on____ the

Chorus

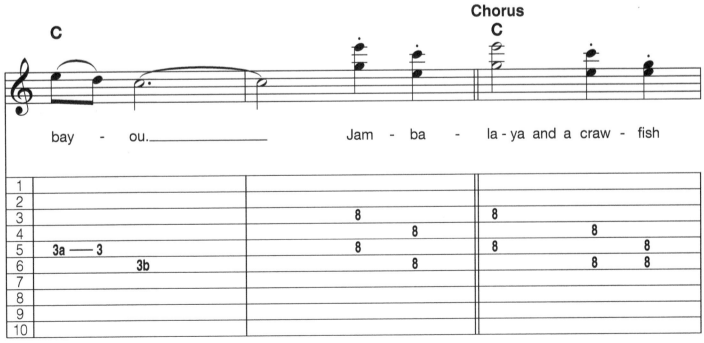

bay - ou._____ Jam - ba - la - ya and a craw - fish

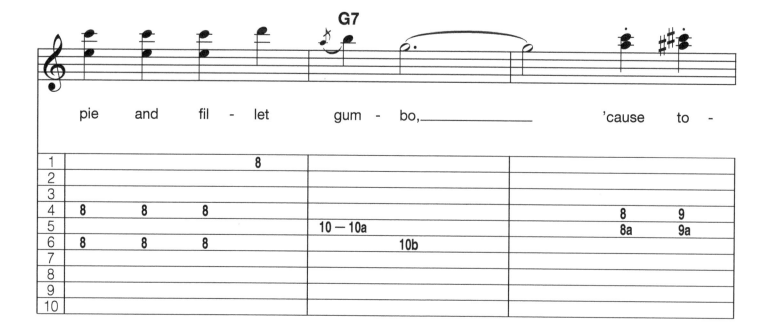

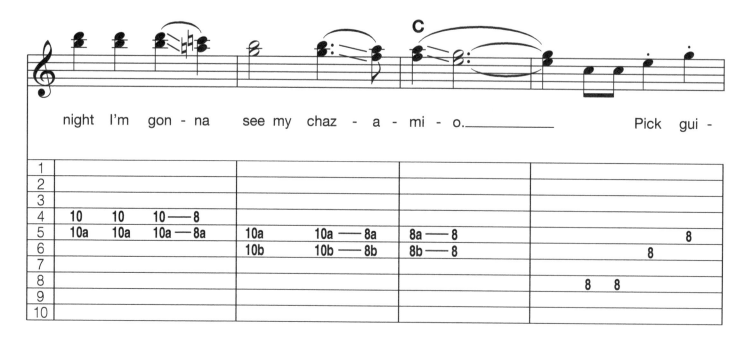

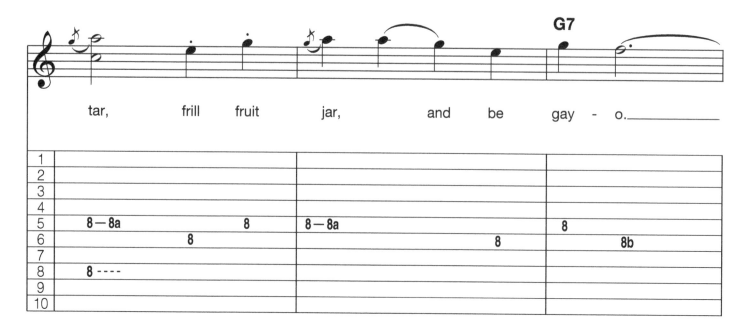

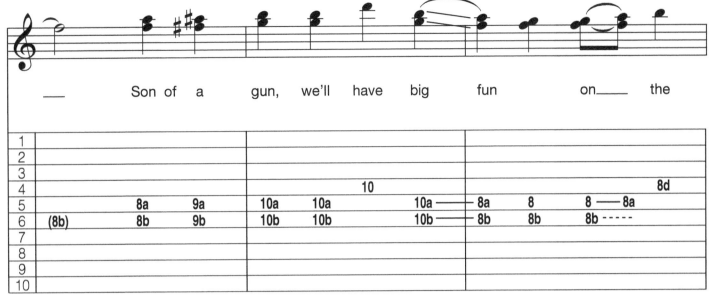

Son of a gun, we'll have big fun on the

Outro

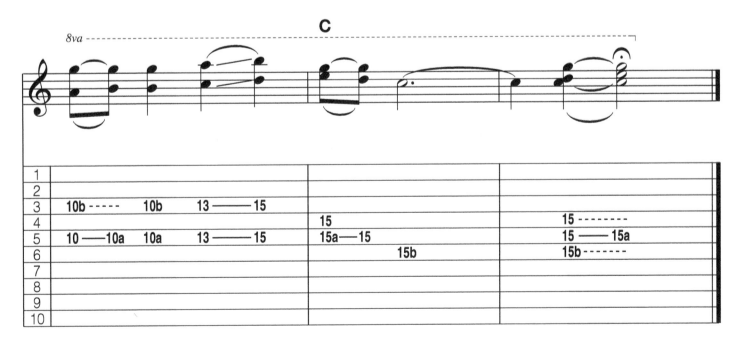

bay - ou.

Take Me Home, Country Roads

Words and Music by JOHN DENVER,
BILL DANOFF and TAFFY NIVERT

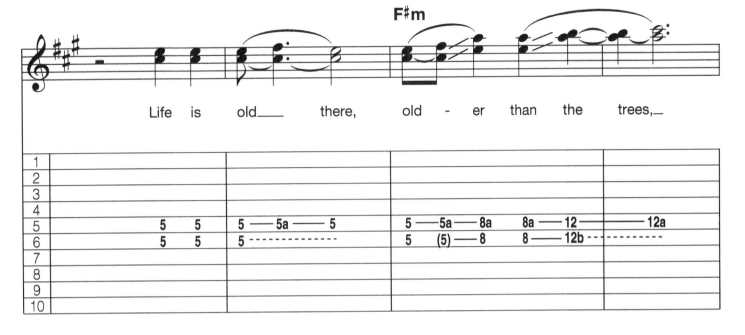

Life is old___ there, old - er than the trees,___

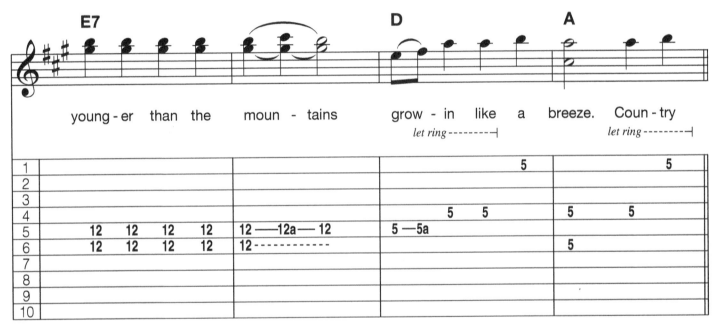

young - er than the moun - tains grow - in like a breeze. Coun - try

Chorus

roads,___ take__ me home,___ to the

Bridge

I hear her voice, in the morn - in' hours she

calls_____ me; the ra - di - o re - minds me of my

let ring ---------------| *let ring -------------------------|*

home____ far a - way.   Driv - in' down____ the

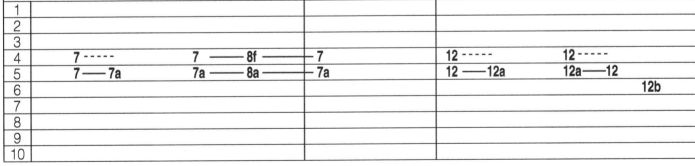

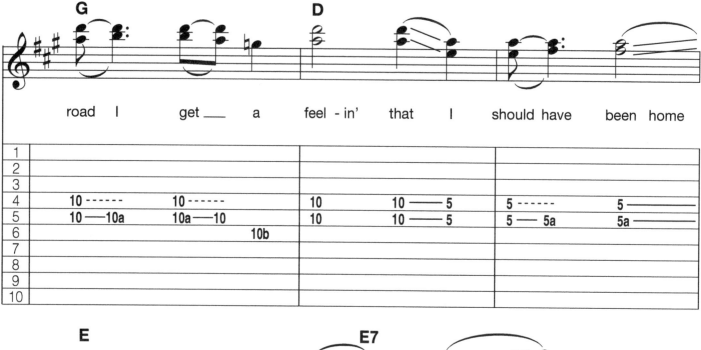

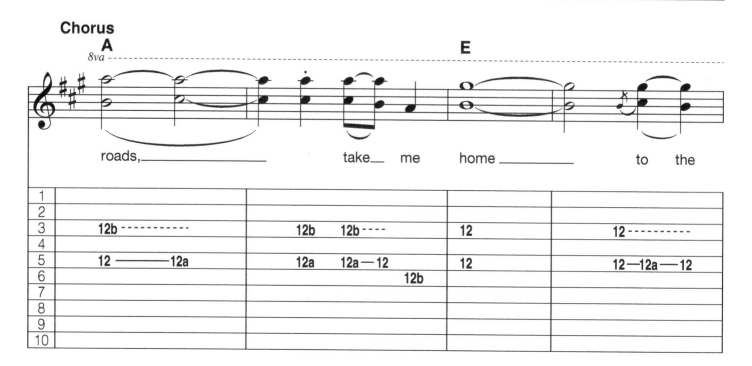

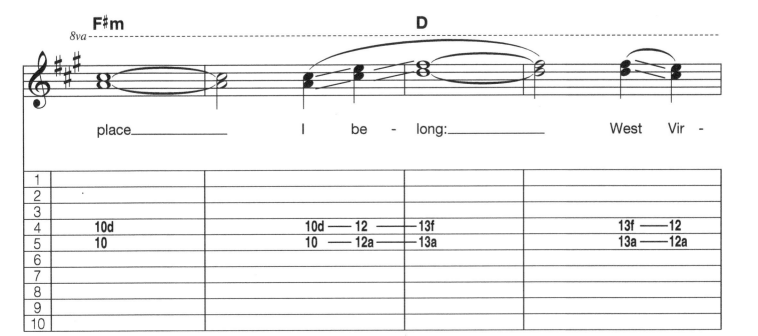

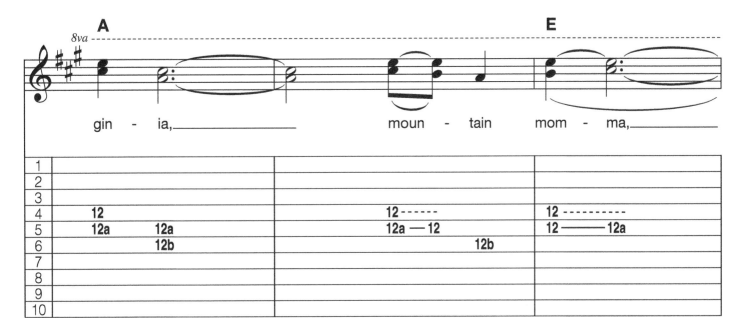

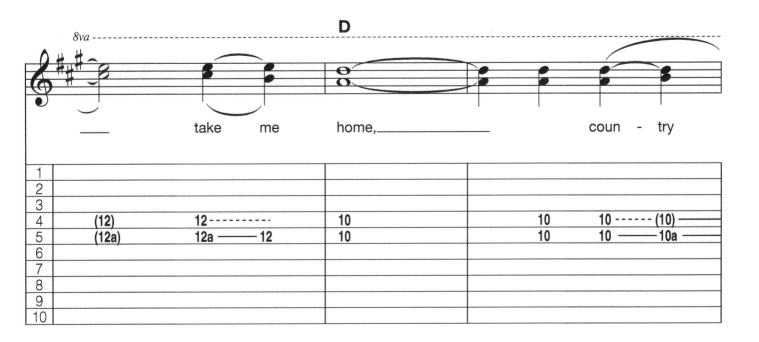

Ring of Fire

Words and Music by
MERLE KILGORE and JUNE CARTER

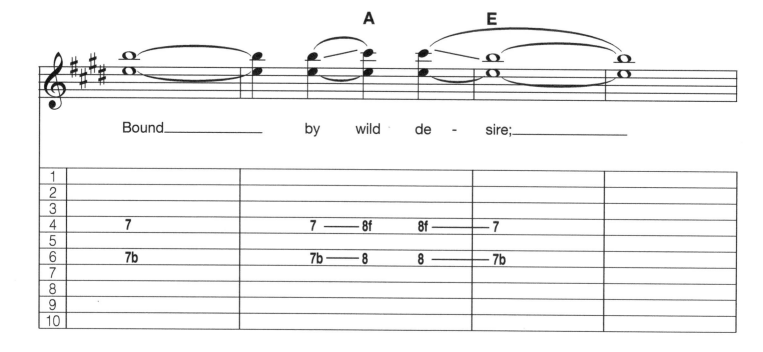

Bound_____ by wild de - sire;_____

1				
2				
3				
4	7	7 — 8f	8f — 7	
5				
6	7b	7b — 8	8 — 7b	
7				
8				
9				
10				

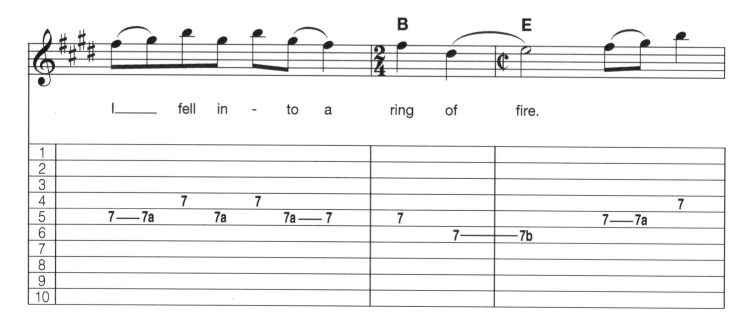

I_____ fell in - to a ring of fire.

1			
2			
3			
4	7 7		7
5	7 — 7a 7a 7a — 7	7	7 — 7a
6		7 — 7b	
7			
8			
9			
10			

Chorus

I fell in - to a burn - in' ring__ of

1				
2				
3	7b			
4			14	12 ------ 12 -----
5		7 10a — 14 — 14a 14a		12 — 12a 12a — 12
6		7 10 — 14b ------		12b
7				
8				
9				
10				

fire. I went down, down, down,__ and the flames__ went_____

1			
2			
3			
4			14	12 ----- 12 -----
5	12	7 ——— 10a	14 — 14a 14a	12 —12a 12a—12
6	12	7 ——— 10	14b - - - - - -	12b
7				
8				
9				
10				

high - er. And it burns, burns,_____ burns,_____

1			
2			
3			
4			7
5	12	7a — 7	7 ——— 7a
6	12	7b	
7			
8			
9			
10			

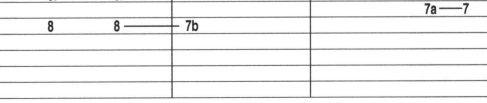

___ the ring of fire._____ the ring___ of

1			
2			
3			
4	(7) 8f 8f ——— 7		
5			7a —7
6	8 8 ——— 7b		7 ———
7			
8			
9			
10			

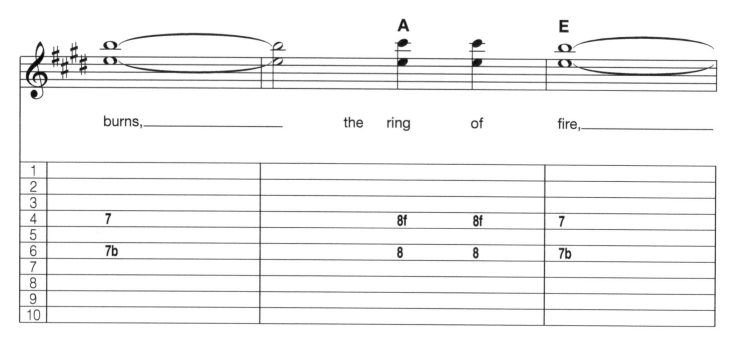

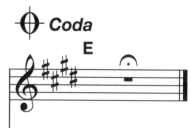

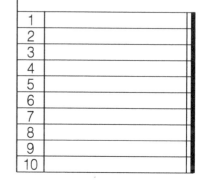

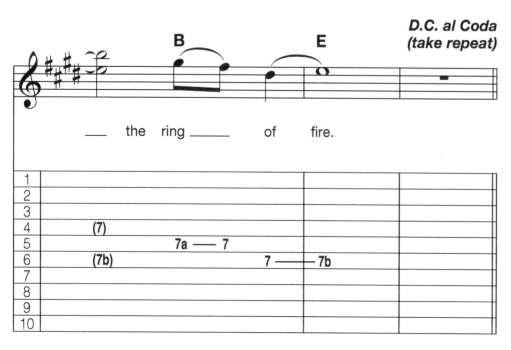

Rocky Top

Words and Music by
BOUDLEAUX BRYANT
and FELICE BRYANT

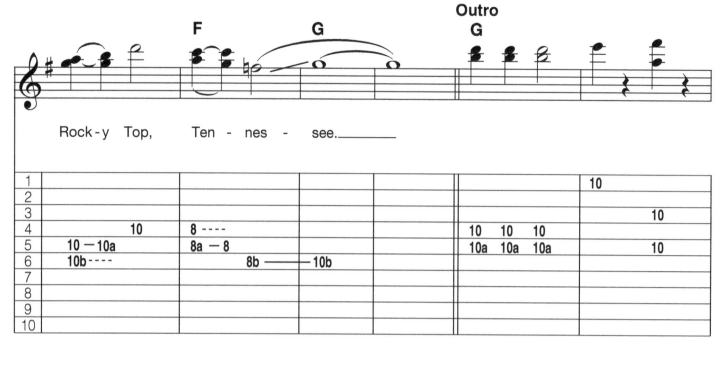

Rock-y Top,   Ten - nes - see._____

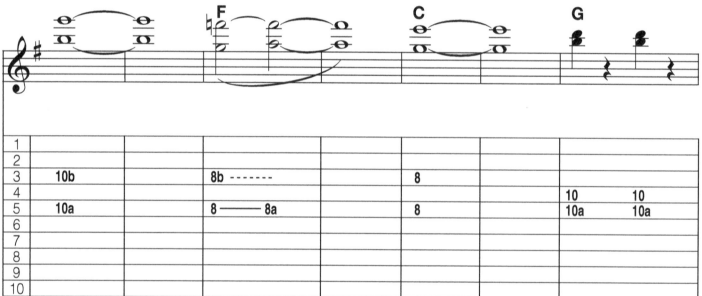

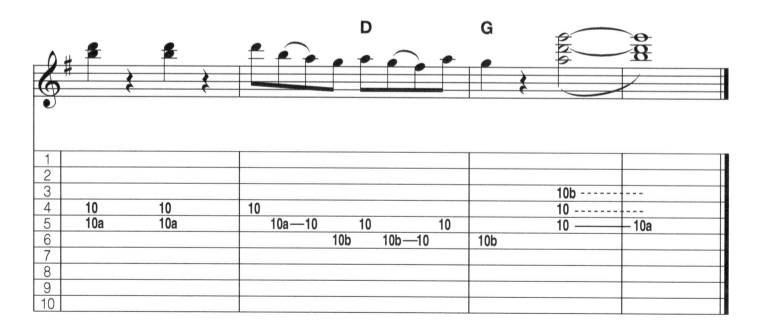